Corporate Culture —
Diagnosis and Change

Corporate Culture — Diagnosis and Change

Auditing and Changing the Culture of Organizations

Desmond Graves

St. Martin's Press, New York

© Desmond Graves, 1986

All rights reserved. For information, write:
Scholarly & Reference Division
St. Martin's Press, Inc., 175 Fifth Avenue, New York, NY 10010

First published in the United States of America in 1986

Printed in Great Britain

Library of Congress Cataloging-in-Publication Data
Graves, Desmond
    Corporate culture — diagnosis and change.
    Bibliography: p.
    Includes index.
    1.   Corporate culture.
    I.   Title
HD58.7.G69   1986   302.3′4   86–3953
ISBN 0–312–16988–4

Contents

Acknowledgements

It behoves the writer of this kind of book to be modest, for he has plenty to be modest about. He only collects facts and expresses views; and if the former are wrong and the latter mistaken he also collects the blame. At every stage in the process he incurs debts to a multitude of kind-hearted people.

I should therefore like to thank, first, the many hundreds of managers and their chief executives who collaborated in the research, and Patience Hilton, Librarian at the Oxford Centre for Management Studies, who helped me with the reading matter from the first day to the last. In interpreting the statistical data my hand was guided by Dr. Paul Griffiths at the Oxford University Computing Service who also re-analysed the data kindly provided by Eric Roughley of the ESRC data archive. Professors Keith Thurley, Pjotr Hesseling and Frank Heller endeavoured to find a few needles of wisdom in the haystack of half-truths. The motivation to complete the work was provided by Doreen Alford, assisted latterly by Heather McCombie — without their gentle chiding the work would have remained unfinished to this day.

The credit for turning the manuscript into a moderately readable book rests with the publishing team led by Peter Moulson who, with the help of Sharon Kelly and the copy editors Heather Bliss and Adèle Linderholm, have enabled the author to put his name to something far better than he deserved.

Finally, I should like to thank my wife, Mary, for her forbearance when more important tasks were left undone, and also my family, Penelope and Robert, Christopher, Catherine and Elizabeth, whose common sense, insight, intuition and skill with words far exceed my own and whose encouragement was invaluable.

This book is dedicated to the memory of the two men who made this study possible: Professor Edwin Ghiselli, who invented the self-description inventory, and Norman Leyland, first Director of the Oxford Centre for Management Studies.

Desmond Graves
Salter Mill
January 1986

Preface

This book is a modest attempt to place the writer's learning and research in the field of corporate culture at the service of the reader, whether he or she be a student in search of essay material, an academic seeking a summary of the literature, a researcher comparing methodologies or a businessman faced with the problem of understanding the culture of his firm. As these four strands are intertwined in the book, some explanation may avoid frustration.

The first chapter is an introduction to the idea of corporate culture — does it exist? If so, is it important? Different reasons for using the idea are given and the purpose of the research —to arrive at a broad taxonomy of organizational cultures — is explained. This should be of some interest to all readers.

The second chapter is primarily for those in search of a summary of the literature on the subject. It attempts a working definition, and most importantly for the student, tries to distinguish between culture (a long-lasting phenomenon) and the more evanescent climate. The second chapter is supplemented by the Appendix, in which other review material may be found.

In the third chapter we get down to trying to compare corporate cultures. One way is to study the way companies reinforce their cultures through senior management training. Four organizations are studied and some inferences drawn as to differences in behaviour, attitudes and values in the sphere of management training.

Chapters 4 and 5 are more for the student than the practitioner. They recount the writer's attempt to deal objectively with the culture problem, using (in Chapter 4) a psychological test applied to over six hundred managers (two hundred of them in the four companies studied in the previous chapter); and in Chapter 5 using the data collected by the Aston Group and now in the ESRC archive at the University of East Anglia. These chapters enable the reader to assess the quality of the work underlying the conclusion in Chapter 7.

Chapter 6 is the distillation of a number of interviews with chief executives of the firms studied, written so as to integrate their views into an anonymous whole. This was not a difficult task, since there are greater similarities between the jobs of chief executives than at any other level of the organization, whether professional, administrative or commercial. Every chief executive has to make a profit for his firm, whether this is expressed by a figure or by some improvement of the quality of life. This is equally true for public and private sectors; only the weighting is different. Studies of chief executives are notoriously difficult to carry out and communicate: they lack the weight of large numbers and the safety net of reference points. Yet they are the key to the culture problem. The culture is propagated by them, for them, and about them: and they are controlled by it.

In chapter 7, there are some generalizations about comparative culture, showing that there is plenty to be modest about. The principal result is to show that the Harrison taxonomy was on the right lines, though unsupported by research and therefore inadequate. This research proposes something a little more sophisticated and points the way towards better understanding of the nature of corporate culture.

There is also some advice about changing the culture, based upon the first-hand experience of organizations undertaking this task. As with all attempts at social change, there cannot be 'one best way' but, at the very least, if you understand where you are going you will know whether you have got there or not.

Finally in Chapter 8, we summarize this research and point the way forward to better understanding of corporate culture.

1 Introduction

Sociologists have long contended that membership of stable primary groups is essential to the well-being of every society. It is through membership of groups that basic needs for affiliation, security and recognition are satisfied. The basic argument has a long history from Durkheim (1933) to Kasarda and Janowitz (1974) who are united also in declaring that the traditional sources of affiliation are disappearing. Perhaps the most discouraging scenario is that painted by Homans (1950) who wrote (p.457):

> Now all the evidence of psychiatry . . . shows that membership in a group sustains a man, enables him to maintain his equilibrium under the ordinary shocks of life, and helps him to bring up children who will in turn be happy and resilient. If his group is shattered around him, if he leaves a group in which he was a valued member, and if above all he finds no new group to which he can relate himself, he will under stress develop disorders of thought, feeling and behaviour . . . The cycle is vicious; loss of group membership in one generation may make men less capable of group membership in the next. The civilization that by its very process of growth shatters group life will leave men and women lonely and unhappy.

To some extent, education for life consists in training people to master the art of superficial adherence to transient groups. Certainly private school education was, and is, aimed at this goal, often creating the stable group to which notional adherence is guaranteed for the rest of life and which often arises out of family instability — the offspring being sent there because the parents are divorced or the father mobile. University may only aggravate the problem since few provide residence for the whole time, and even then in changing accommodation. Small wonder that workpeople at managerial levels seek the benefits of group membership by joining an organization in which they will find what life does not normally afford — status, esteem and security.

Often the workplace acted as an encapsulant from society as described by Lipset, Trow and Coleman (1956), Trist and Bamforth (1951) and Gouldner (1954). At other times it embraced society, such as in the Selznick study of the TVA (1949) and Abegglen's study of the Japanese factory (1958). In each case a new culture was created at the workplace with its own morality, its own standards. It has been popular to decry such efforts to recreate what society has abandoned (e.g. Whyte (1956)) as contrary to man's inalienable right to be an autonomous individual. Observers have not been slow to remark upon the effect of dual loyalties on family and social life. Yet companies whose culture is unashamedly paternalistic, such as IBM, have no difficulty in recruitment, whilst in companies where there is no special attempt at socialization, members are now slow to create norms that they subsume under the general category of corporate culture. Several studies of implantation of one culture into another indicate that people like working for a 'foreign' firm with highly developed cultural elements, and not only for any extra money it might bring (see, for example, Johnson and Ouchi (1974)). If we accept that organizational culture in some sense compensates for psychological gaps in society, then we must also study the environment in which such an organization exists. For instance, an organization that expects its managers to be mobile must provide a supportive culture, whereas one which employs its managers at the same site for their entire careers may not (unless it is asking them to work unsocial hours). In studying paternalistic American companies, Ouchi and Jaeger (1978) shows that their culture consists of a modified form of Japanese corporate culture, as follows (Japanese stereotype in brackets):

Long-term employment	(Life-time employment)
Consensual decision-making	(Same in Japanese model)
Individual responsibility	(Collective responsibility)
Slow evelation and promotion	(Japanese similar)
Implicit informal control with explicit formalized measures	(Japanese similar, but no measures)

| Moderately specialized career paths | (Japanese non-specialized) |
| Holistic concern including family | (Japanese similar) |

Apparent discrepancies between actual behaviour and culture norms are explained via the 'mock vs. real' device used by Gouldner (1954) to describe the bureaucracy in the gypsum mines. Yet they remain paradoxes. Can one join an organization which is dangling, as bait, one set of values and yet remain for quite other reasons? In this book we shall be looking to see whether individual and organizational values are distinguishable and, if so, why certain types of person join certain organizations.

In attempting a 'systems' explanation of organizations, Margulies and Raia (1978) looked at various sub-systems that underlie the general system. Among these is the 'cultural sub-system', which includes:

> such things as informal organizations and status hierarchies. It consists of a set of values about what should and should not be, what is and is not important, and other generally shared views. It also consists of normative ideas about behaviour which are usually accompanied by rewards and punishments designed to reinforce the norms. [p.13.]

They distinguished culture, which 'develops and changes slowly over time' (p.14) from climate, which is 'more like a weather barometer. It is a reflexion of the day-to-day relationships between people, and between people and their jobs'. According to them, the climate consists of activities, interactions and attitudes which lead to 'trust or mistrust, collaboration or competition, mutual support or parochialism, open or closed communication' (p.13). Later they devoted some space to advocacy of the importance of changing the cultures to change behaviour, without, however, giving much detailed evaluation.

In considering the factors affecting culture we may look at two different approaches:

1. *The structuralist view*

   The 'building bricks' here are the size and shape of a group or organization, the degree of formalization and centralization, the span of control, the role and the status structure.

   There are two subsets of this category of theorists: the 'holistic structuralists', who look at the organization as a whole (e.g. Weber, and particularly Pugh *et al.* (1969)); and the 'psycho-social structuralists', who attempt to discern and emphasize the structural elements of the group, such as Whyte (1957), and Homans (1950).

2. *The interactionist view*

   Into this category we may place those scholars whose preoccupation is with process and relatedness. There are again two subsets: those for whom the social system is crucial, such as Emery and Trist (1965) or Katz and Kahn (1966); and those who are more concerned with rationality, even if bounded, such as March and Simon (1958), Cyert and March (1963) and Dill (1978).

The consideration of the approach to corporate culture for each area leads to sets of statements which are highly questionable, such as:

1. The culture in a large organization is always different from that in a small one.
2. The culture in a participative organization is always different from that in a non-participative one.
3. The culture in a well-articulated organization is always different from that in a badly articulated one.

The first proposition would appear to be self-evidently false: there is no obvious reasons for people to act differently in a large organization from the way they act in a small one, unless control systems are linked to size and also impinge upon the job to a greater or lesser extent.

The second proposition has a *prima facie* validity. But such a distinction proves unhelpful because participation in itself is not a measure of organization choice since some jobs do not permit of participation, as we shall see later from Bowers' investigation.

The third proposition implies that the degree of logic in the articulation of the organization is important for its culture. A logically designed organization is seen as different, culturally, from an illogical one. But how can people within such organizations know this? Is it through a sense of purposiveness, or attention to tasks? In this case we might examine the process of profit-maximization. In each organization we may find that the culture does not reflect logical structure but rather the perceived importance of the methods of control, of technology and of profitability itself. In human terms we can measure the culture according to what proportion of the managers are apparently task-orientated, highly skilled and greatly in need of reward. Such an analysis could lead us to think that a firm like IBM had a strongly marked culture (rating high on each dimension) while other firms had a somewhat weaker culture because their organizational logic was not clearly spelt out.

Given the partiality of these approaches, it becomes necessary to look for an approach to corporate culture that stands beside but is not subsumed by purely theoretical attempts to describe and explain a phenomenon that, according to Silverman (1970) and others, may, like beauty, only exist in the eye of the beholder. In the sections that follow three such approaches will be examined to see how far they can provide a framework for investigation.

Culture as a behavioural process

Payne and Pugh (1976) described climate as

the characteristic behavioural processes in a social system at one particular point in time. These processes reflect the members' values, attitudes and beliefs which thus have become part of the construct. Given climate's geographical analogy, the organizational context and structure variables are the hills and rivers or physical features of the geographical area. Climate dimensions such as progressiveness and development, risk taking, warmth, support and control correspond to temperature, rainfall and wind velocity which have been generated by the interactions of physical features with the sun's energy. Social systems' equivalent energy sources are people who also create and are part of the climate. Although both physical and social climates may affect their respective structures, the context and structure of a social system are more stable than its people whose energies may not always be spent in predictable cycles. [p.1126–1128].

The problem with such a definition is that it ascribes a different quality of reality to context and structure on the one hand, and people, 'the energy source' on the other, as if context and structure were themselves proof against people.

However, the concept of climate is not without value, since it leads to the study of countervailing forces and the relationship between the quest for autonomy *and* homonomy emphasized by Angyal (1941) and conceptualized in a dynamic model of national culture by Graves (1970).

Angyal suggested that the life process as a whole was interpreted as the resultant of two forces: the autonomous determination of the organism and the heteronomous influences of the environment. He argued that 'the individual tends to go from a state of lesser autonomy to a state of greater autonomy'. In other words, the person has a tendency to master the environment and, by conquest and achievement, to impose his will upon a widening realm of events. The concept of a trend towards increased autonomy is closely related to the technical concept of 'aggression' (p.375). At the same time there is a tendency to desire to fit into the organizations of society, such as the family or social group.

He argued for a holistic study of personality that takes into account the relationships between man and his environment. The study of culture, which he defined uncontroversially as 'a socially inherited body of sanctions and directives which define the "proper" and "improper" ways of behaviour' (ibid., p.379), could help to highlight the whole *gestalt*: on the one hand it forms the complex environment to which one has to adjust; on the other, being assimilated by the individual, it functions as part of the super-ego and conditions his tendency to autonomy.

In drawing attention to the concept of the biosphere he stressed interdependence and rejected sciences that attempt to segmentalize the study of man. The science of personality he sought to propound was one relating to the 'physiologically, psychologically and socially integrated total process of living'.

A dynamic model can be derived to explain cultural differences. The model (Fig. 1.1) illustrates the dynamic tension referred to by Angyal in that it shows how one tendency was corrected by the opposite influences. It was devised to explain behavioural differences between English and French managers (Graves 1970).

	England	*France*
Primary thrust towards:	Autonomy	Authority
Unit of social construction:	Person	Role
Social force:	Centrifugal	Centripetal
Countervailing thrust:	'Fair play' norms	'Alienation' detachment

Figure 1.1 *Behavioural model*
Source: Graves 1970

This view of culture as a homeostatic process rather than a static model has not been questioned or controverted — at least not in public. However, the concept has remained only partially operative, for two main reasons:

(1) It did not allow the placing of other cultures within its framework, except along a continuum. This is probably a fault of presentation rather than anything else, since study of other cultures would undoubtedly provide similarly dynamic homeostatic models (for instance, the Japanese culture might be thought of as a culture of consensus, where the main concept is the group; the main problem is loss of identity, and this is remedied by fear of failure). The heavy cost in terms of research investment of getting even to the stage of analysing one culture almost completely precludes replication in other cultures and since it was produced there has only been one methodologically sound cross-cultural study (Hofstede 1981) and since that took place in a firm with its own strong organizational values, its results require cautious interpretation.

(2) The model was dichotomous but the behaviour reported was only bi-modal. The 'soft' data (interviews) threw up a constant

stream of exceptions to the cultural rules. It was possible to observe extremely role-based attitudes and behaviour and extremely person-based attitudes and behaviour in both cultures. By comparing the three sets of data the researcher came to the conclusion that homonomic behaviour was more likely in France than in England, but there were plenty of qualifications to be made. At the end of the day the model was usable more as a general dichotomy about two main organizational types than as a model for understanding cross-cultural differences. To quote Angyal (1941, p. 7) again:

> The utility of a theory consists essentially in that it serves as a guide, as a point of reference, for empirical studies, which otherwise are likely to result in an utterly chaotic and incoherent mass of data. The utility of a good theory is twofold: it allows us to question nature intelligently and offers a background for the interpretation of empirical data.

In the intervening years since the first study, little has been seen which enables the problem of culture in management to be significantly better understood.

Within cultures the state of research is hardly better developed. With the exception of Harrison's (1972) work, few useful maps of business culture have been created — and this despite the ever-growing flood of organizational climate studies (as summarized in such articles as Hellriegel and Slocum (1974), Payne & Pugh (1976) and Nicholas (1982). The reason for this is probably that the technology of culture measurement tends to have been developed to solve the problem of improving productivity or satisfaction, with the usual attempt to be prescriptive that so trivializes behavioural science research.

The only attempts to create experimental environments that have received widespread notice are Lewin, Kippitt & White (1939) and, following them, Litwin & Stringer (1968). Here again the tendency is prescriptive, founded on a 'human relations' approach to managing that currently attracts almost as much invective (e.g. Rose (1975)) as did its predecessor, the Classical School, now coming back into favour as recession and under-privilege once again pervade the world.

Given this state of affairs, it becomes desirable to test the model in a more bounded environment. The hypothesis may be stated as follows: if it is true that different cultures create different attitudes and behaviour patterns, and if it is true as Haire *et al.* have said (1966) that the cultural element is a substantial but not overwhelming conditioner of behaviour, then significant differences between the attitudes and behaviour of people in different organizations indicate the presence of something we may call organizational culture, that is, (following Eldridge & Crombie (1974)) 'the unique configuration of norms, values, beliefs and ways of behaving that characterise the manner in which groups and individuals combine to get things done' (p.89).

An early attempt to do this was made by Bowers (1969). In a study to examine the relationship of organizational climate to managerial behaviour in twenty-four organizations, he claimed that 'organizational climate appears to account for about one-third of the variance in managerial leadership regardless of the kind of organization' (p.20). This large conclusion is based upon some Likert-type assumptions about the nature of organization behaviour as being the interactive behaviour of interlocking groups who 'impinge upon one another'. In his definition, organizational culture consists of five variables:

Communication
e.g. How receptive are those about you to your ideas and suggestions?

Motivation
e.g. How much do you look forward to coming to work each day?

Decision-making
e.g. To what extent are the persons who make decisions aware of problems at lower levels in the company?

Control
e.g. How much say or influence do the various levels of the hierarchy have on what goes on in your department?

Co-ordination
e.g. To what extent do persons in different departments plan together and co-ordinate their efforts?

These five climate variables were then correlated with four leadership variables, as follows:

(1) Managerial support i.e. The degree to which the manager 'increases his subordinates' feeling of being worthwhile and important people' (p.9).

(2) Goal emphasis i.e. The degree to which the manager 'stimulates enthusiasm for getting the work done'.

(3) Work facilitation i.e. The degree to which the manager 'helps his subordinates to get the work done by removing obstacles and roadblocks'. (p.6).

(4) Interaction facilitation i.e. The degree to which the manager 'builds the subordinate group into a work team'.

It will be seen that (1) and (4) deal with the employee as an *organizational* participant, whilst (2) and (3) deal with the employee as a member of a *production* team.

Bowers argued that those ways of behaving are handed down from group to group and so constitute the culture of the organization. He found that 30 to 50 per cent of the variance in managerial behaviour related to the impact of the five climate indices, and that the best single predictor was usually as good as the combined correlation. Overall, this was 'communication', although in the case of the automated fabrication industry, 'motivation' was more important. He found that the other three factors (decision-making, control and co-ordination) made little difference. 'In fact,' he concluded, 'once the combined impacts of communication and motivation are accounted for, the net impact of the remaining decision-making variance would appear to be negative, not positive' (p. 20). If this were true, we would have to concentrate on key variables such as climate-builders, for example, utilizing drives and climate destroyers, for example, individual decisiveness and autonomy.

'Decisive' people destroy organizational cultures because they do not allow 'custom and practice' to weigh in a decision, and this is why we are strongly aware of culture as constraining activity in heavily traditional organizations such as British trade unions.

In a later re-analysis of the same data, Taylor and Bowers (1972) found that there were four main indices of organizational culture and two tentative ones. These were as follows:

Human resources, primacy of	e.g. To what extent is this organization really interested in the well-being of its employees?
Communication flow	(as previously measured)
Motivational conditions	(as previously measured)
Decision-making practices	(as previously measured)
Technological readiness to change	e.g. To what extent is this organization quick to use improved work methods?
Influence of lower levels	(previously 'control')

Co-ordination is now replaced by primacy of human resources and readiness of the organization to change technology. However, as these items are difficult to measure objectively we cannot say the argument has been advanced by the massive reclassification of data. The model thus remains relevant to the study of organizational change but is not very helpful for discriminating between organizations, although, as we shall see, Ellis and Child (1973) have endeavoured to carry the matter further.

Organizational culture as a means of stabilising behaviour

Continuous attention to goals that are constantly changing could be extremely disruptive to an organization that does not possess the loose matrix structure commonly associated with the high technology area of industry. Angyal (p.55) has stated that 'it is not the goal that defines direction, but on the contrary the intrinsic pattern of direction which defines what object can become a goal'. More recent work by the Chandler school has not convincingly rebutted that statement.

From this point of view culture might be seen as the glue that holds organizations together — a means by which participants communicate and co-ordinate their efforts — and incidentally a ring fence separating insiders from outsiders (see e.g. Kramer (1974) and Foy (1974)).

Porter, Lawler and Hackman (1975) have stated the argument as follows:

> Organizational 'culture' [is] a set of customs and typical patterns of ways of doing things. The force, pervasiveness and nature of such modal beliefs and values vary considerably from organization to organization. Yet is is assumed that an organization that has any history at all has developed some sort of culture and that this will have a vital impact on the degree of success of any efforts to alter or improve the organization. The organizational behaviour literature is replete with illustrations of developmental attempts that have failed due to insufficient attention in advance to the prevailing culture. Of course, if these cultures were completely immutable then no change undertakings would be successful. So the point is not that an organization's culture cannot be modified but rather that if development is to take place, its chances for success will be improved by taking into account the prevailing and dominant norms and values that already exist in the situation. The recognition on the part of the members of the organization that there is a predominant culture that can be identified is presumed to be a significant factor in facilitating and ensuring the survival of meaningful changes [p.489].

Their guarded language conveys a scepticism that is generally felt by organizational researchers, for when attempting to define its elements we fall back upon such awkward concepts as those used by Albrook (1967):

Leadership
Motivation
Communication
Decision-process
Specificity of goals
Degree of control.

Earlier in their work they advise the consultant working on Organizational Development programmes to 'make haste slowly'.

In other words, culture is more of a constraint on planned change than a conscious set of norms and objectives. In this book we shall attempt to examine this proposition, and then test it in terms of data collected about people in organizations.

Thompson (1967) has analysed the paradox of organizational administration, where some degree of certainty in operation has to be maintained alongside flexibility in seeking out new opportunities. 'Paradoxically, the administrative process must reduce uncertainty but at the same time search for flexibility' (p.158). He resolved the paradox by pointing out that *certainty* is important in the short run, and *flexibility* in the long run. He avoided defining the two terms. He went on to suggest that 'the central part of the administrative hierarchy, the managerial layer, would become the translator, securing from the institutional level sufficient commitments to permit technical achievement, yet securing from the technical core sufficient capacity and slack to permit administrative discretion and, if necessary, recommitment of resources' (p.150). It is in this area that the invocation of organization culture as a rationale can be useful as a stimulus for action. Hedberg, Nystrom and Starbuck (1976) have also seen the dual purpose of culture — a benchmark against which to measure need for change.

Thompson also argued that since managers always tend towards the reduction of uncertainty, the rationalization of action as explicable by organization culture will enable action to take place (p.153). Cultures also enable common ground to be established when coalignment of different cliques becomes necessary (p.147). It is interesting to note that in his book he does not mention or discuss the concept of organization climate or culture, preferring to treat it as the implicit dependent variable of the administrative system.

If this is all true, then culture simply exists as a bench mark for organizational change, induced as the cause of organizational malfunction. Change is justified by inappropriate culture, as Burke (1972) stated forthrightly. According to his view, organizational development is 'a planned sustained effort to change an organization's culture.'

> From what type of culture to what other kind? From a closed culture, characterised by decision-making vested in authority of position; inflexibility of organisation structure; and one reward system . . . to a culture of openness: decision-making as a function of authority of expertise, competence and information: flexible organisation structures adaptive to changing needs and functions: and a variable reward system, in which employees have choices. [p.63.]

One would hardly accuse this author of Taylorism, yet the last statement, the only one in which people are mentioned, comes remarkably close to it! At least, however, Beckhard states two alternatives, if only in structuralist–functionist terms.

A more cautious position was taken by Hofstede (1980) who preferred to say that:

> in general we find that outstandingly successful organizations usually have strong and unique cultures: the successes themselves contribute to the company mythology which reinforces the sub-culture. Unsuccessful organizations have weak indifferent sub-cultures or old sub-cultures that become scelerosed and can actually prevent the organization's adaptation to changed circumstances [p.394].

Unfortunately, he did not define strength: but we shall endeavour to test this hypothesis when we compare the companies involved in the research, and we shall see that three of his four variables are important elements in their cultures.

Hunt (1981) questioned the Hofstede approach. Having attempted to interpret Hofstede's data in the light of common cultural beliefs about centralization and formalization and emerging with a taxonomy relying on these two dimensions, he laid bare the central problem of the work:

> His concentration on one multinational compels us to ask whether he is studying the culture of the Japanese or French or British of

Malaysian executive or the culture of a multinational firm. For example, training officers who believe their packages are suitable for all cultures may, in fact, be producing a corporate culture that overrides local values — even to the extent of being in conflict with the culture of that society. [p.62.]

Lorenz (1967) has explained the need for culture in social organizations as follows:

> In cultural ritualisation, the two steps of development from communication to the control of aggression and from this to the formation of a bond are strikingly analogous to those that take place in the evolution of instinctive rituals . . . The triple function of suppressing fighting within the group, of holding the group together and of setting it off as an independent entity against other similar units is performed by culturally developed ritual in so strictly analogous a manner as to merit deep constraint. [p.65.]

He continued as follows: 'any human group which exceeds in size that which can be held together by personal love and friendship depends for its existence on these three functions of culturally ritualised behaviour patterns' (pp.65, 66).

The three functions he speaks of in terms of animal behaviour provide exactly the answer to the general question: why do organizations need culture? Without the cultural rituals it would be impossible to distinguish one from another; it would be impossible for long to counteract the entropic tendency and it would be difficult to contain the conflict created by structural behaviour. Lorenz proceeded to talk about norms of behaviour. 'Everything that is called manners is, of course, strictly determined by cultural ritualisation' (p.66). This led him to a discussion about verbal and non-verbal communication that reinforced, albeit from a different point of view, the arguments of those who view communication as the chief element of culture. (See, for example, Schall (1983).)

Organizational culture as an incentive to commitment by falsification of the equity balance

Adams (1963), following Homans (1961) and Jaques (1961), has argued that membership of and performance in organizations continues for so long as there is seen to be a balanced ratio between inputs and outcomes as compared to those of others in the organization. Imbalance causes the individual to

(1) Perceptually change inputs or outcomes, or
(2) Actually change inputs or outcomes, or
(3) Leave the organization

It is quite easy to see how, given a perfect labour market, with everybody's inputs and outcomes exactly similar, the mobility of labour would be high. Organization culture may enable people to accept that a cognitively unfavourable work bargain is psychologically attractive for them because the culture somehow raises their input of work to a greater level of meaning (because the organization 'understands' them) and the outcomes are more salient for them because the organization, which is an extension of their personality, is somehow enhanced. The outcome may not be intrinsically valuable to the individual (such as a pay rise), but it may have an instrumental value (the turnover increases). However, this is by no means certain: the individual may also feel overborne by the culture and use it as a reason for physically or mentally 'opting out'.

Adams' proposition has support from many, e.g. Chinoy (1951), Hearn and Stoll (1975), Kramer (1974), Staw (1974), who found that people stayed in their jobs even though the jobs did not meet their requirements. In the laboratory, Rosenberg (1960) has demonstrated that by changing affect toward certain objects through hypnotic manipulation of his subjects, they changed in both perceived instrumentality and in their value statements regarding these objects. Cognition may shape affect, but affect can also shape cognition.

We may therefore treat organizational culture as a stabilizing force that acts to maintain behavioural direction when expectancy/equity conditions are not met and do not function. Since this is exactly the definition of organizational commitment worked out by Scholl

(1981), it follows that culture is the mirror image of commitment, and therefore represents the investment of the organization in the individual member, just as commitment is the investment of the individual in the organization. We may then examine how the organization makes its investment and how it balances investment with return, in terms of high commitment and reduced propensity to leave for 'better things'. Scholl identified (p.593) four commitment mechanisms: investments, reciprocity, lack of alternatives and identification. Each of these can be used in the organizational culture context by implementation of a personnel policy that creates dependence upon the organization as a kind of 'perpetual parent' or one which encourages freedom of mobility between organizations.

Such an approach would, however, involve the examination of formal company policy — the way it is created and communicated, and the degree of adherence to it. Then would come an examination of the customs and practice of the organization — the way things get done. This would be followed by an examination of symbols and ways of indicating identity. Such subjective matters are difficult to evaluate because of the twin problems of salience and variability. They can only, at best, provide circumstantial evidence: attempts to place them at the centre of cultural descriptions prove to be inconsequential, as Chapter 2 will try to show.

Wiener and Vardi (1980) have further advanced the argument by showing that work behaviour is a function of motivation (a calculative concept) and commitment (a normative value-based concept). Kiesler (1971) suggested, furthermore, that attitudes and values are generally formed so as to be consistent with behaviour: thus culture may be the means by which the organization manages to secure long-term membership, by enabling the employee to rationalize his continuing long-term membership of the organization despite an equity imbalance.

Organizational culture as a defence against anxiety

De Board (1978) assessed the evidence for treating organizations as social defence systems. He cited Jaques' (1955) hypothesis that within the life of an organization the defence against anxiety is one of the primary elements that binds individuals together. Maladaptive behaviour such as hostility and suspicion observable in organizations is the social counterpart of the symptoms that an individual might exhibit through projection. 'In this sense, individuals may be thought of as externalizing those impulses and internal objects that would otherwise give rise to psychotic anxiety and pooling them in the life of the social institutions in which they associate' (p.479). He subdivided these defences into those against paranoid anxiety and those against depressive anxiety. Some examples are cited, mainly from Jaques' (1951) experiences at Glacier Metal, and Menzies' (1970) case study of a hospital.

The conceptual framework underlying this view of organizations is that of Klein (1959) who advanced the twin psychological mechanisms of projective and introjective identification, whereby the person blames bad attributes on the outside agent and takes the good attributes upon himself.

This analysis may be of use in explaining phenomena such as poor interpersonal relations within firms, although the basis of their business is good client relationships (such as insurance brokers) and emotional refusal to use management techniques in organizations whose main business is science-based. According to this line of argument the culture would be the scapegoat for failure and the organization could be blamed for behaviour seen as dysfunctional by outsiders. It is indeed noticeable that criticisms by outsiders of cultural quirks are hotly resisted until the outsider is accepted by the organization as understanding its deeper purpose, when the criticisms are themselves accepted, even welcomed. Provided the organization is seen as 'good', the 'bad' parts can be admitted. This is not dissimilar to a psychotherapeutic approach, but a simpler approach might simply be to say that people look to the organization to compensate for deficiencies in their own personality, and in so doing become dependent upon the organization, thereby aggravating rather than resolving their personality problems, and, worse still, deforming the personalities of new entrants. As Menzies (1970) concluded:

The needs of the members of the organisations to use it in the struggle against anxiety leads to the development of socially structured defence mechanisms which appear as elements in the structure, culture and mode of functioning of the organisation. A social defence system develops over time as the result of collusive interaction and agreement, often unconscious, between members of the organisation as to what form it will take. The socially stuctured defence mechanisms then tend to become an aspect of external reality with which old and new members of the institution must come to terms. [p.10.]

Organizational culture as a system of causal relationships

Although not mechanistically orientated, Hudson (1978) advances a didactic theory that helps us to understand organizational culture homeostatically by viewing each characteristic in three ways (p.92).

(1) What is its origin?
   The origin of a characteristic is a reaction to an environmental need such as survival, efficiency, growth reliability.
(2) What is its function?
   The function will be to cause people to subscribe or contribute to the organization, in return for some reward such as pay, security or power.
(3) What is its consequence?
   The consequences may be desirable, such as conformity, or undesirable, such as dependence and loss of initiative.

An analysis, along these lines, of organization culture may be performed deductively (beginning with the environment) or inductively (beginning with the individual). The latter method enables us to visit each of the sub-parts of the culture independently before seeking the key variable that makes the whole culture recognizable. As Hudson points out:

The number of rival interpretations you can place on a

given body of evidence is in principle limitless. What matters in practice is that the interpretation you offer should be a 'good' one. It should pick out aspects of the material that seem pertinent. It should be accurate, internally consistent, and, if possible, intelligible . . . It is not enough simply to produce a story that is *compatible* with the evidence — a story that is usually, in effect, an extension of its teller's bountiful ego. It must constitute the *best* reading — the reading that captures most succinctly what the evidence has to say. [p.25.]

Hudson seemed to be saying that we must integrate all our knowledge of culture until the lines lead, like the Vredeman de Vries' perspective drawings, to a central point which we may call the cultural cornerstone.

Organizational culture as operant conditioner

Skinner (1971) had much to say about the conditioning effect of the environment. While not denying the autonomy of man (and neither does the organizational folklore), he showed how it is a relatively limited autonomy. He saw the culture as a constantly adaptive mechanism, enabling its inhabitants to survive and yet forcing them to develop in a way that enabled the culture itself to survive. Skinner pointed to three ways in which culture may be designed (pp.148–49):

(1) To reduce disturbance and increase autonomy.
(2) To increase well-being and reduce power.
(3) To increase efficiency and survival.

Much the same may be said of organizational cultures.

However, the analogy breaks down when we come to examine the possibilities of the conscious design of culture, advocated by Skinner, because we are not able to proceed deductively. Although we know that for reasons of security people would like organizations to survive, yet they do not always act to keep them in being. Cases where employees accept reductions in wages in order to keep the organizations alive are rare enough to be newsworthy, and such cases are usually in the artistic sector. Skinner's conclusion that 'it is science or nothing, and the only solution to simplification is to learn how to deal with complexities' (pp.157, 158) is a false battle cry because it is philosophy, not science, that enables man to deal adequately with complexities. His warning about the danger of simplification leading to superstition is just, but there is a third way — and that is the one we shall follow. For organizations, like cultures, must embrace people of diverse natures in order to survive, and this seems to limit the amount of control available.

What is it that conditions operants in organizations? According to Schein (1983) we must look at all the constraining mechanisms that guide or mould behaviour, such as:

(1) Formal statements of organizational philosophy.
(2) Design of physical spaces, façades, buildings.
(3) Deliberate role modelling, teaching and coaching by leaders.
(4) Explicit reward, status system and promotion criteria.
(5) Stories, legends, myths and parables about key people and events.
(6) What leaders pay attention to, measure and control.
(7) Leader reactions to critical incidents and organizational crises.
(8) How the organization is designed and structured.
(9) Organizational systems and procedures.
(10) Criteria used for selection, promotion and retirement of people. [p.22.]

As will be seen, many of them are long run (such as (2)) or handed down through the senior management (such as (5) and (7)), so that they become very difficult to measure. Others, while easier (though not much easier) to measure are not always reliable, such as (8). It is easy to see why there has been, in recent years, a sudden increase in research on myths and legends: they are fun to collect and analyze. Unfortunately, they are not easy to use in a comparative setting.

The chief conditioning process is often thought to be the character and motivations of the leader. In the next section we review some examples of such studies.

Conclusion

It can be seen that the concept of organizational culture illustrates a common dilemma in efforts to describe and understand human behaviour. The basic problem is how to define and operationalize the concept in order to measure it reliably and validly. There is considerable although not unanimous agreement that the concept is meaningful — in that it has important implications for the comprehension of human behaviour in organizations. However, there are many critics of the methodology used. Johannesson (1973) has argued that because of the nature of the methodology and the underlying quest for a link between culture and job satisfaction 'perceptual measurement of climate runs the distinct risk of turning out to be little more than an alternate form of measurement of job satisfaction'. (pp.37-7). This view has been endorsed by Guion (1973) and James and Jones (1974), among others.

Tagiuri (1968) has pointed out that behavioural science has long had problems with 'environmental' concepts such as organizational culture, and has summarized the most important of these problems as follows:

(1) Distinguishing between the objective and subjective environment.
(2) Distinguishing between the person and the situation.
(3) Determining what aspects of the environment need to be specified.
(4) Identifying the structures and dynamics of the environment. [p.13.]

These problems remain pertinent to the study of organizational culture today and to a large extent are still unsolved. One way of avoiding these problems might be to study the personal characteristics of the organizational members using an objective measure. This frees the person from his context, and limits the consideration of relevant aspects of the environment to those affecting recruitment. Then the fourth problem is solved by an assessment of the environment itself.

Managers feel strongly about organizational culture but until now have had few ways of talking about it, still less of measuring it. As Harrison has pointed out:

An organization ideology obviously has a profound effect on organization effectiveness. It determines how decisions are made, human resources are used and the external environment is approached . . . An organization ideology tends to be internally viable when the people within the system want and need the prescribed incentives and satisfactions that reward good performance. It tends to be externally viable when the organization it embodies is a microcosm of the external environment and rewards the same skills, values and motivations. [p.123.]

There is a further possibility of testing the strength of the ideology if the needs and values can be measured.

Such emphasis upon the interplay between personality and environment was also mentioned by Forehand & van Haller Gilmer (1964) who added some of the reservations that will be dealt with in the final chapter of this book — as follows:

(1) It is necessary to compare comparable organizations.
(2) It is not certain that organizations are homogeneous units.
(3) Climate is a dynamic not static concept.
(4) The climate is a *Gestalt*, and not a dimension.

The attempt to define the climate of an organisation raises . . . the question of the way in which dimensions are best combined to describe a particular organisation. A meaningful combination may be a linear one but it seems more likely that it will be a pattern or configuration. [p.378.]

This book will try to arrive at a broad taxonomy for organization cultures. It will also suggest, following Silverman and Jones (1976), who worked in one of the organizations studied, that one key to 'culture' is management selection.

A possible model for understanding organizational culture may look something like Figure 1.2.

In what follows, the literature of organizational culture will be evaluated and shown to be overly preoccupied with job satisfaction (a prime example being Lawler *et al.* (1974)). Then the findings from over 600 Ghiselli pro formas will be described and analyzed to see

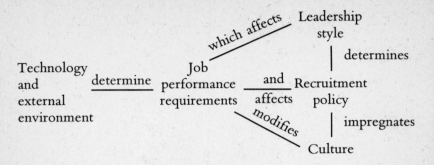

Figure 1.2   *Model of determinants of culture*

how far they give both general and organizational culture-specific information. Finally, an attempt will be made to justify the model shown in Figure 1.2, in which culture appears as a constraining variable upon job performance. It will be noticed that this model ignores the variables of structure and authority much researched by the school of thinkers led by Pugh. This is because they are treated as imaginary artefacts of the culture — a kind of negative print of which culture is the positive. As Bacharach and Lawler (1980) say, 'organizations are politically negotiated orders . . . they are the result of the conscious political decisions of particular acts and interest groups' (pp.1, 2). The work of Pugh and the structuralists will be discussed in Chapter 8.

2. What are we talking about?

So far, we have shown that the literature is bedevilled by two difficulties: lack of clear definition of the terms 'climate' or 'culture' and lack of rigorous experimentation to assess the concept. In the first part of this chapter we review some attempts at definition, and then examine some theories of culture.

It is, perhaps, appropriate to begin with a series of papers edited and written by Tagiuri and Litwin (1968) under the general title *Organisational Climate — Explorations of a Concept*. In attempting a definition of 'climate', Tagiuri says (p.24) 'it is, in fact, difficult to give a general, formal definition that is not too trivial or nearly useless because it encompasses too much.' After an exhaustive review of other definitions he arrives at the following:

> Organisational climate is a relatively enduring quality of the internal environment of an organisation that (a) is experienced by its members, (b) influences their behaviour, and (c) can be described in terms of the values of a particular set of characteristics (or attributes) of the organisation. [p.27.]

This definition begs more questions than it eliminates: for instance, what is the length of the relatively enduring quality? And how can we distinguish climate from other influences upon behaviour? And what is the value of a particular set of attributes? The difficulties about this approach are highlighted by another paper in the same collection by Meyer who measured climate along six dimensions:

— Constraining conformity: the *feeling* employees have about the constraints in the office . . .
— Responsibility: the *feeling* that employees have a lot of individual responsibility delegated to them . . .

— Standards: the emphasis that employees *feel* is being placed on doing a good job . . .
— Reward: the degree to which employees *feel* that they are fairly rewarded for good work rather than only being punished when something goes wrong.
— Organizational clarity: the *feeling* that things are pretty well organized rather than being disorderly, confused or chaotic . . .
— Friendly team spirit: the *feeling* that general 'good fellowship' prevails in the atmosphere, that management and fellow employees are warm and trusting, and that the organization is one with which people identify and are proud to belong [sic] . . .

The words 'feel' or 'feeling' occur in each dimension and create some doubt as to whether such subjective assessments, leading out of the definition invented by Litwin, can have any value, since feelings can change in the very short term, influenced by the economic or political environment. For instance, a motivation instrument based upon Maslow's hierarchy of needs showed that achievement and self-realization needs were the most salient until the 1974 slump, when financial and security needs became more salient, almost overnight. In some ways (e.g. needs for reward, security and affiliation) Meyer's dimensions represent a rearrangement of the Maslowian need hierarchy. As will be shown later in this work, however, the needs are themselves created by the work environment rather than satisfied by it.

In quotations illustrating the different meanings attributed to the word 'climate', Tagiuri quoted, *inter alia*, McGregor (1960) as follows:

The day by day behaviour of the immediate superior and of other significant people in the managerial organisation communicates something about their assumptions concerning management which is of fundamental significance . . . Many subtle behavioural manifestations of managerial attitudes create what is often referred to as the 'psychological climate' of the relationship. [pp.133–4.]

This is a proposition capable of being tested since we can examine the ways in which people behave in given situations in different organizations. But we should not assume that it is the behaviour of the 'significant people' in the organization that creates the culture: rather, they are its manifestation and the means by which it is communicated. This proposition has already been tested by the writer in terms of national culture (1970); the purpose of this book will be to hold the national culture constant and vary the organization culture, assuming with Hofstede that national culture transcends organizational culture (despite the fact that many of his findings do not seem to support this.)

Evan (1968) tried to establish a relationship between organization climate and culture. He found some evidence to suggest that culture may be the more appropriate term, but for his purpose found the term 'culture', with its connotations of beliefs, values and norms, too broad. He noted the Margulies' description of the 'outer' culture, which is defined as 'the degree to which the organization is capable of adapting its dynamic environment' (p.109), but commented that 'this conception [sic] is not distinguishable from the concept of 'organizational flexibility' nor did it capture the subjective or perceptual dimension conveyed by the term. From our results it would appear that there is both an objective and subjective culture — the one which is observable and the one which colours the orientation of the individual. They serve different purposes and may be differently evaluated. Indeed, this appears in Evan's definition (p.110) which runs as follows: 'Organizational climate is a multi-dimensional perception of the essential attributes or character of an organizational system.' He was not the only sociologist to prefer the perception to the reality and used the term 'multi-dimensional' to emphasize that perceptions of all observers should be taken into account. The rest of his article was devoted to the creation of a 'system model' of organizational climate in which he showed that perception by others of the climate affected their interactions with it, and the climate itself was the intervening variable between the experience of the organization by its members and the performance of the organization in pursuit of its goals. In other words, he explained variability of performance between organizations solely in terms of climate. This is a large assumption.

Moreover, his testable propositions which will be reviewed in Chapter 5 of this book, are interesting since they relate to the mismatch between external and internal climates. If the internal climate is more comfortable to members than the external, there would be low motivation to change, and vice versa. This, however, is a syllogism because the two climates are measured upon different dimensions (subjective and objective) so there is little possibility of reliable comparison. However, in his peroration (p.122) he made three typically commonsense recommendations which have been followed here:

(1) Concentrate upon values, interpersonal relations and tasks.
(2) Prefer a comparative approach.
(3) Attempt development of scientific instrumentation.

He concluded: 'The labour involved . . . is indeed formidable, but unless progress is made in operationalizing the concept of organizational climate it will remain a common-sense rather than a social science concept.'

Numerous other definitions of culture have been put forward which resemble one another only in their vagueness. No single element is detachable that might enable the culture to be measured. For instance, Krech *et al.* (1962) have defined culture as

the pattern of all these arrangements, material or behavioural, which have been adopted by a society as the traditional ways of solving the problems of its members. Culture includes all the institutionalised ways and the implicit cultural beliefs, norms, values and premises which underlie and govern conduct. [p.380.]

French and Bell (1973) defined culture as 'prevailing patterns of activities, interactions, norms, sentiments, (including feelings), beliefs, attitudes, values and products (p.16).

Later, Margulies and Raia (1978) defined it more simply (p.90) as 'the commonly shared beliefs, values and characteristic patterns of behaviour that exist within an organisation' without saying what

constitutes 'characteristic'. However, they used the term inter-
changeably with 'system', talking about a formal culture and an
informal culture.

A more oblique but more testable definition has been given by
Guion (1965). Quoting Ohmann's (1958) reflections upon the nature
of managerial authority, he says

> the attitude of those highest in our organization towards such
> propositions determines in large part the 'organizational climate'
> in which managers and their subordinates must function. That
> climate may emphasize work or personal loyalties and relation-
> ships; it may be democratic or authoritarian; it may stress
> consideration in leadership or highly structured organization at
> each level. A manager must work within the climate of his own
> organization. [Here followed examples of the effect of mismatch
> between the managerial style of the person and the climate of the
> organization.] The impact of organizational climate upon
> managerial behavior does not necessarily come from above.

Summarizing, he writes:

> [A manager] succeeds or fails according to the technical,
> intellectual and social skills he can bring to his job and according
> to the degree to which he can fit into the climate of the job and
> satisfactorily resolve the conflict he finds in it. [pp.463–4.]

What the nature of this conflict is we are not told; it may be the
conflict between the norms of the organization and its needs to
develop. Certainly culture can be invoked in turbulent times to
avoid certain paths of action and favour others, the latter being more
'in keeping' with the culture and, as Perrow (1979) has put it,
'shaping the world as one wishes it to be shaped' (p.13).

Later in this chapter we shall review the progress made in
this direction since these words were written.

So far we have reached the stage where the term 'organization
culture' seems more appropriate than 'organization climate' because

it brings into consideration the question of salience of the various environmental stimuli. In this we are supported by Eldridge and Crombie (1974) who wrote as follows:

> Culture . . . is a characteristic of all organisations through which, at the same time, their individuality and uniqueness is expressed. The culture of an organisation refers to the unique configuration of norms, values, beliefs, ways of behaving and so on that characterise the manner in which groups and individuals combine to get things done. The distinctiveness of a particular organisation is intimately bound up with its history and the character-building effects of past decisions and past leaders. It is manifested in the folkways, mores, and the ideology to which members defer, as well as in the strategic choices made by the organisation as a whole. The individuality or cultural distinctiveness of an organisation is attained through the more or less constant exercise of choice, in all sections and levels. . . . The character of organisational choice is one of the major manifestations of organisational culture. [pp.89–90.]

In considering culture, Eldridge and Crombie drew attention to three dimensions, following Angyal (1941): depth or vertical dimension; breadth or lateral co-ordination of the contributing parts; and the progression dimension which refers to co-ordination through time. They elaborated as follows:

> The depth dimension is exemplified in the formulation and adoption of policies, programmes, procedures and practices that represent the basic values and strategic commitments of the organisation as a whole — the inducement of behaviour at the 'surface', in the day-to-day organisation functioning, that are compatible with and serve to further basic values that are embodied in the organisation. [p.96.]

Dysfunction along this dimension would result from the interruption of the logical ladder steps from ideology to implementation.

So far as the lateral dimension was concerned, they stated simply that this refers to the problem of 'coordinating disparate courses of action in the direction of mutual consistency and ensuring at the same time that they support the achievement of the aims as a whole' (p.96). This does not tell us much about culture and its role in integrating rival parts of the organization. Indeed, the culture may well point to the reverse behaviour.

With the third dimension they were scarcely happier. They mentioned the temporal spread of activities, and hint that culture should help to produce consistency, but when it comes to the point they relapse into remarks about planning 'research and development and so on'! Finally, they attempted to give as an example the socialization of the military recruit so that he will 'choose appropriate courses of action almost spontaneously' (depth), make contingency plans (progression) and co-ordinate his activities with other units (lateral). The example is a bad one. The military climate is of compliance with routines, and to see the military organization as a feedback mechanism flies in the face of the evidence produced by Dixon (1976), amply supported by many case histories. Dixon showed that military commanders, far from profiting from the climate, are more often victims of it: 'Prejudice, ignorance, fear of failure, over-conformity and sheer stupidity may disrupt leadership decisions as surely as they interfere with planning or technical decisions' (p.34). He later pleaded for more intelligent military systems but submitted that this runs counter to the climate:

. . . along with all the other psychological problems which beset those whose business is organised violence is that of deciding whether to plump for intellect or character as the means whereby instinct is controlled and discipline maintained. Generally speaking the older military organisations have opted for character and the younger ones for intellect. [p.197.]

These may provide us with two kinds of culture: one where the predominant variable is that of the leader and another where the predominant variable is that of the system, and there may be combinations of the two.

To test this proposition we would need to find organizations where the variance between the environment and organization activities could be explained by tangible aspects of organization culture. The aspect of 'progress' would be shown by assessing the rate of change from one state to another.

Finally, Eldridge and Crombie revised their definition:

> We come to the view therefore that an organisational culture is a dynamic complex system, characterised by constant adjustments in its internal relations, changing relations with elements in the environment, and increasingly required to adapt to changes taking place in the relations among the elements of the environment themselves. [p.99.]

Thompson (1967) has drawn attention to the 'homogenizing influences of culture' (p. 102) — the tendency within societies to socialize all individuals in the direction of certain dominant standards, beliefs, values and expectations. It is against this touchstone that organization theories are judged and evaluated.

Serving the needs of the organization may prove an acceptable excuse for behaviour that would normally be condemned by the culture. For instance, Millgram (1974) quoted one observer of his experiment in which people think they are administering dangerous electric shocks to helpless victims in the furtherance of science:

> I observed a mature and initially poised businessman enter the laboratory smiling and confident. Within twenty minutes he was reduced to a twitching stuttering wreck who was rapidly approaching the point of nervous collapse. He constantly pulled on his earlobe and twisted his hands. At one point he pushed his fist into his forehead and muttered 'Oh God, let's stop it'. And yet he continued to respond to every word of the experimenter and obeyed to the end. [p.377.]

However, we would not expect such aberrant behaviour to continue over the long term, except that we know that behaviour is tolerated by members of business organizations that would not be acceptable elsewhere.

In addition to general culture, we may further limit the range of the climate in terms of the technology (e.g. need for precision); structure (e.g. degree of co-ordination); definition and allocations of roles (e.g. leadership) and locus of control or degree of regulation. In a seminal article Marenco (1968) has written of high-powered and low-powered organizations and these elements may provide a link with the concepts of control mentioned by Eldridge and Crombie. Whereas they use control in the sense of overlords exacting predictable behaviour from underlings and point to the deleterious consequences, we must treat control as a simple variable which we can observe and measure, noticing meanwhile that participants whose behaviour is most closely controlled by the organization (e.g. civil servants) most resent external controls (e.g. by government).

In the end we are forced to the conclusion that Eldridge and Crombie are not able to define culture in a form in which it may be measured, although they do give some clues about where it may be seen to cause differences, e.g.:

Technology — demanding or low-geared?
Structure — complex or simple?
Roles — clearly defined and bureaucratic or unsystematic and patrimonial?
Control — overt or suppressed?

Before looking at the research carried out in the field, it is relevant to examine at least some of the theoretical and analytical contributions that have been made.

Theories of culture

In an interesting paper dealing with the relationship between climate and behaviour theory, Litwin (1968) examined three main theories of individual behaviour and related them to four main theories of organization behaviour. Each of the theories of individual behaviour sheds a little light upon the relationship between worker and organization.

In psychoanalytically derived theory, Litwin stated, 'the concepts of object–choice and object relations are basic to an understanding of the relation of a person to his environment' (p.36) and quoted Freud (1915–49) as follows: 'When the object becomes a source of pleasurable feelings, a motor tendency is set up which strives to bring the object near to and incorporate it into the ego; we then speak of the attraction exercised by the pleasure-giving object and say that we "love" that object'(pp.79–80). Thus, if certain objects in the organization culture were seen to be salient we may then expect them to be internalized by the employee who will then share them with other employees as part of the culture. These objects would be pleasurable, such as pay, security, status and so forth. Litwin noted, however, that 'there is relatively little systematic psychoanalytically based analysis of the environments people have to deal with, or of how different types of environments are organized and dealt with' (p.37). It is clearly much easier to evaluate the environment in laboratory experiments than in the firm, and it will be the task of this book to trace the significant element or elements of the environment from the descriptions of themselves provided by the inhabitants of the organization culture. In this way we shall fulfil Litwin's request (p.38) for an attempt to 'conceptualize or treat systematically the nature of environmental influences.' An important element of psychoanalytically derived theory to which Litwin did little more than allude is the concept of transference. Litwin did not mention that perhaps the main *raison d'être* of the climate concept is the need for actors to justify some sense of purpose in their activity and to legitimate their needs and drives. Organization people need to obtain both enhancement and protection from their environment and this is why, as we shall see, it is possible to distinguish an inner as well as an outer environment.

Litwin turned next to the concept of environment in stimulus–response theories of organization, beginning naturally with Pavlov (1927) and moving to the work of American psychologists led by Hull (1943) who advanced theories as to the relation between stimulus, response, habit and reward. In environmental terms, the value of the theory would be to draw attention to the degree of conditioning in the culture exemplified by the amount of prescriptive behaviour and hence the strength of the culture. Here the requirements of the technology for exact responses may play a large part. Litwin, however, pointed out that the theory is essentially molecular and even atomic, and culture is a molar concept so that in order to make use of this theory it would be necessary to look at a large series of events and trace them back to some simple key stimulus; otherwise the various behaviours may become self-cancelling and randomized. As Litwin said (p. 40), 'the organism's responses to the set of physical stimuli making up the environment are treated mechanically, with no consideration of selective perception or subjective evaluation'. As we shall see, this ignores the general cultural profile generated by the cultural nerve-centre of the organization.

The third set of theories addressed by Litwin is expectancy-valency theory, as discussed principally by Tolman (1926) and Atkinson (1964). Here again the same criticisms apply as to stimulus–response (S–R) theory, except that at least the accent falls upon subjective expectations rather than objective behaviour and to this extent the theory becomes easier to handle because less prone to generalization. Furthemore, we are able to distinguish between the objective environment as perceived by detailed observers and the range of behaviour or attitudes envinced by the actors, and factor analysis will give several explanations of the sort of person who is likely to be attracted to, and conditioned by, one organization rather than another.

This discussion leads (somewhat artificially, since it is wellnigh impossible to discuss *Hamlet* without the Prince) to a review of field theory itself and Lewin's (1935) statement that 'only by the concrete whole which comprises the object and the situation are the vectors which determine the dynamics of the event defined' (pp.29–30). Field theory is an attractive explanation for human behaviour which has lost nothing in the telling by its admirers, except the possibility of rigorous testing. Lewin does, however, help us in this case by making the useful distinction between figure and field:

To characterise properly the psychological field one has to take into account such specific items as particular goals, stimuli, needs, social relations, as well as such more general characteristics of the field as the atmosphere (for instance the friendly, tense or hostile atmosphere) or the amount of freedom. These characteristics of the field as a whole are as important in psychology as, for instance, the field of gravity for the explanation of events in classical physics. Psychological atmospheres are empirical realities and are scientifically describable facts. [1951, p.241].

Unfortunately, he does not say how this may be done; but in our examination of the psychological climate from primary sources, we shall be trying to compare the organizations in our sample using the specific items he mentions. Even if we cannot be sure of describing the organization accurately we can use what has been called 'distal focusing', in other words the historical, economic, social and technological fields or contexts within which the organization nests, thus enabling general distinctions to be drawn between each.

Litwin then proceeded to an examination of the various organization theories in terms of the effects of the environment upon behaviour. While this is an interesting exercise, it need not concern us at this moment, except for his conclusion that due emphasis should be placed upon structure, technology, norms, salience and leadership, since each of these items is used by more than one of the different schools of thought.

In summary, it is clear that Litwin saw the need for technical methods of evaluating the environment and that he was baffled in the attempt because he began at the wrong end — the environment — rather than asking, as we have done, what people consider to be their internal models of themselves, and then connecting these with the environments they inhabit.

A way through the problem is suggested by Sells in the same volume. He suggests (p.87) that 'organizational climate appears to be a function of the culture patterns of organizations and to include these generalized orientations of members which are (a) shared by a majority of members of an organizational unit, and (b) acquired in relation to factors specific to the organizational situation'. In plain language he suggested that we should study what people do, what values they hold, where these values come from and how they create organizational bias. This is not new, and all parts will be attempted in this book.

His paper, although difficult to operate, as are so many research prospectuses, contains ideas from Parsons which can form the basis for an investigation of business organizations. They are:

(1) Adaptation
How has the organization changed over time, and in response to

which stimuli? If we can answer this, we shall understand what stimuli the individual considers to be significant.

(2) Goal attainment

What goals does the organization set for itself and how are these transmitted? What are the criteria for success? Who monitors this success and how is it improved?

(3) Pattern maintenance

What value systems and philosophy will be used to enforce conformity? Does the organization have a 'hair-shirt' or 'silk-shirt' mentality? Does it have expressed rules of fair play?

(4) Integration

How are the people and functions homogenized? What steps are taken to ensure the uniformity of culture patterns throughout the social system? How much autonomy is encouraged, and is this a spurious value ('we like our people to be rugged individuals') or a real consideration ('we are more interested in results than methods')?

Sells in his paper suggested a highly elaborate taxonomy which is too detailed for our present scope and what we have done is to reintegrate some of the more important terms into the fourfold Parsonian structure so as to produce a workable framework for our investigations of the firms.

Our hypotheses will be that (1) the sub-populations of each firm have discernible different characteristics, and (2) these characteristics may be attributed to beliefs about the way the firm expects them to behave for the attainment of their own life-goals.

To paraphrase Crozier (1965), the sociologist is not interested in whether the soup is good, so much as who drinks it, and what effect it has upon his behaviour. To this extent we have to rely upon the Thomas theorem quoted in Merton (1957), 'if men define situations to be real, they are real in their consequences'.

More recent thinking has elevated the notion of culture from the status of variable, whether dependent or independent, external or internal. The word begins to be used as a metaphor for conceptualizing organization. Smircich (1983) has identified five intersections between organization theory and what she calls culture theory, as follows:

(1) In *classical management* theory, culture is an instrument serving human biological and psychological needs.
(2) In *contingency* theory, culture functions as an adaptive-regulatory mechanism, and unites individuals into social structures.
(3) In *cognitive* organization theory, culture becomes a system of shared cognitions. The human mind generates culture by means of a finite number of rules.
(4) In *symbolic* organization theory, organizations are seen as patterns of symbolic discourse, and culture is a system of shared symbols and meanings.
(5) In *transformational* organizational theory, where organizational forms and practices are the manifestations of unconscious processes, culture is a projection of the mind's universal unconscious infrastructure.

In other words, instead of something an organization *has*, culture is something an organization *is*. The arena for debate is moved from the intersection of culture with other facets of organization theory to the way in which culture, now defined as the social manifestation of the organization's collective unconscious, defines organization. While this does, as Smircich says, legitimate (in some sense) 'attention to the subjective interpretive [sic] aspects of organizational life', it does not bring us any nearer useful theories or taxonomies for comparative culture.

This is demonstrated by a recent attempt to work at this level of analysis by Riley (1983), who used structuration theory to analyze the political currents of two firms. 'Structuration theory is a metatheory whose principal goal is to connect human action with structural explanation in social analysis' (p. 415). This somewhat mystifying statement is further amplified: 'Structuration, then, is the production and reproduction of social systems through the application of generative rules and resources.' For a complete explanation we are referred to Giddens (1979) who explains:

> A social system is thus a structured totality. Structures do not exist in time–space, except in the moments of constitution of social systems. But we can analyse how deeply-layered structures are in terms of the historical duration of the practices they recursively

organize and the spatial breadth of those interactions. The most deeply-layered practices constitutive of social systems in each of these senses are institutions. [p.65.]

The conceptual framework to which structuration theory leads is, interestingly, unconnected to the countable part of the organization. The structures are analyzed into basic elements of signification (codes, practices), legitimation (norms) and domination (authoritarianism), while the symbols are analyzed as verbal (e.g. myths, jokes, legends), active (e.g. rituals, strategies) and material (e.g. status symbols and furniture). An example of a material symbol expressing a legitimation norm would be the statement: 'When you're promoted you have to dress the part.'

Riley compared a non-routinized firm with a routinized firm (which she defined in terms of its client base) and on the basis of twenty interviews with each firm deduced that while the statements were often somewhat similar, nevertheless there were distinctions to be drawn; the major distinction between the two organizations was in the relative or absolute use of power.

It is all too easy to view this kind of research as inhabiting the lunatic fringe of the field, written in language by turn esoteric and slangy, concealing the paucity of humble inquiring thought, and ending in pathetic banalities such as this (p.435): 'What is most intriguing about organisational culture is the influence it has on the lives of those who live and work within its confines'. Yet even studies at this level can produce insights requiring further consideration. For example, an organization that promotes an image of teamwork while 'legitimizing' (sic) internal competition may not have a 'glitch' in the organization. It may actually be a control mechanism produced by the element of contradiction — there may be just enough interplay between the structures for the organization to maintain its teamwork public image while simultaneously using competition as an individual motivator. In this case both internal and external political actions may benefit the organization.

The trouble with such research is that it is interpretative and not analytical; it presents a descriptive picture without analyzing underlying causes. By treating organizational policies as salient and primary it forgets that organization politics is, at the limit, the means by which things are done (or prevented): it is not the *raison d'etre* of the organization.

The literature is not rich in taxonomies of organization. Since Harrison's first attempt in 1972, to which we shall return later, little thought seems to have been given to the comparative analysis of organization culture. In 1973, Ellis and Child published a thoughtful paper showing that manufacturing organizations seemed to have significantly different characteristics from service organizations; and that within this distinction it was possible to identify organizations with high and low variability of product and technological environments. They suggested (p.238) that 'different industries are typified by different organizational work environments . . . ' and alluded to the consequential problems of selection and management development.

Quinn and Rohrbaugh (1983) also developed a four-stage typology based upon three dimensions — structural control versus flexibility, internal focus versus external focus and concentration upon means or ends. It should be stated that the variables were derived from an analysis of criteria that organizational theorists and researchers use to evaluate the performance of organizations. The results of their investigations indicate that there are links between structure, view of organizations and salience of one particular function. Since effectiveness is largely a subjective measure this approach might be fruitful if comparative measures could be evolved. Their analysis shows that each type of organization may be means-dominated and ends-dominated and the change from one to another may be a cultural dynamic related to stability, while the structural changes may relate to size and introversion/extroversion may be related to market turbulence. However, at this level we would be considering subjectively once more the view organization members took of their organization, and the answers received would probably depend upon the position the member held in the organization. For example, a salesman is likely to see his firm as more ends-related, more externally focused and less flexible than a corporate planner. The model would probably tell more about the differences between parts than the overarching similarities. However, the approach should certainly not be lightly disregarded, since, as they said:

the criteria have traditionally been either selected and then imposed on the organisation by the researchers or evaluators themselves, or they have been derived from interviews with members of the target organisations. In either case, the selected criteria usually reflect an unarticulated but fundamental set of underlying personal values about the appropriate emphases in the domain of effectiveness. These personal values that motivate the choice of particular criteria ultimately underlie the resulting effectiveness dimensions 'uncovered' by (but actually antecedent to) factor analytic studies. [p.365.]

Kilmann (1983) has made a less ambitious attempt, using published material, to classify organizations according to emphasis upon the technical or social system and degree of openness or closed-ness. In this case the attempt to fit every continuum into one framework causes the framework itself to become almost meaningless. He indicated that each of his four systems had its special macro and micro designs, decision processes and influence process. Some of the 'controllable variables', as he called them, are shown in the following table, 2.1.

This brief statement of some of the variables points to certain problems with the model. For example, bureaucratic structures do not create coercive power, nor is the leadership style necessarily coercive. The decision-making is likely to be as incremental as it is computational. This is an example of too many cooks screening out the flavour of the broth.

Table 2.1 *Kilmann's four types of system*

System	Structure	Decision-making	Power style	Leadership style	Jungian cognitive style
Closed Technical	Bureaucratic	Computa-tional	Coercive	Tell	Sensation Thinking
Open Technical	Dual	Judgement	Expert	Sell/consult	Intuition Thinking
Open Social	Organic Adaptive	Increment-alism	Referent	Consult/Join	Intuition Feeling
Closed Social	Informal	Group centred	Referent	Join	Sensation Feeling

Table 2.2 *Bion and cultural styles*

Group fantasy	Time perspective	Means/goals specificity	Pervasive style
Fight/flight	Past (short term)	Means defined Goals ill-defined	Insular
Dependency			Charismatic
a) Strong leader	Present and future	Goals and means	Autocratic
b) After leader	Past (short term)	Neither	Bureaucratic
Pairing	Future (long term)	Goals but no means	Democratic

Kilmann might have remembered to include a reference to Bion's three group states: this service is performed by Kets de Vries and Miller (1984) who tried to show that organizations are more or less fixated in one of the states. Incorporating a somewhat odd distinction between culture (shared ideals, values and beliefs) and climate (interpersonal behavioural uniformities that result from the shared fantasies and their derivative culture — p.113), they associated Bion's three states with four styles. In order to do this, they distinguished between dependent organizations with and without a strong leader. Table 2.2. shows three organizational dynamics, somewhat different from Kilmann's.

Again, it is difficult to recognize a framework for allocation. The inference from Table 2.2 must be that only organizations having a dependency relationship with a strong leader are likely to have specific means and goals in both present and future; this surely is the province of the bureaucratic organization. Yet, according to these authors bureaucracy yields only short-term perspective. Furthermore, Bion was interested in these states as products of one another, not as steady states, and to construct a meaningful theory using Bion it would surely be necessary to consider, as he did, the basic assumptions underlying the state. The theory would become more insightful if the authors had been able to make such statements as 'the organization is aggressive (fight/flight) because the basic assumption is the dominance of the leader (dependency) and the counter culture is pairing'. Such statements, if justified, might lead to a consideration of the dynamics of culture, including internal and external culture. However, the restrictive definitions used give rise to only one set of conditions of behaviour.

However one may criticize it for simplicity the Harrison (1972) model provides one realistic solution to the problem of creating a taxonomy that can be related easily to the structural elements, human values and external conditions. Based upon the Tannenbaum-Schmidt power continuum, it hypothesised four basic cultures. The first, 'power-type', entails strong centralized leadership and conforming behaviour by subordinates. In such a climate a good deal of conflict is to be expected, but mainly of a 'vertical' nature. It is likely that the structure of the organization will be poorly defined, with power wielded by the man at the top. In the role-type organization power is still concentrated into a few hands, but the role structure is clearly defined. In such bureaucratic cultures alienation and self-seeking are apparent and there is relatively less commitment to organization goals. Harrison's third type, called the 'task culture', is meant to describe those organizations where emphasis is laid upon consultation and co-operation rather than coercion or the exercise of authority. Harrison saw a good deal of creativity arising out of the proper exercise of task culture. Finally, the 'atomistic' culture is the one where there is little formalization and little attention paid to the leader, even if one exists. It approximates to the 'garbage-can' theory of management, with accents placed upon randomness rather than order.

These four cultures can be integrated using the two basic building blocks of organization — centralization and formalization. Power-type cultures evince centralization but not formalization; task-type cultures are formalized but not centralized; role-type cultures are both; and atomistic cultures are neither. Furthermore, it is possible to conjecture that task-type cultures (typically using a matrix-type structure) and atomistic cultures are more a prey to the vicissitudes of the market-place than the more rigidly bureaucratic role culture or the individually controlled power culture, and it is possible to show that as organizations develop and become less market-dependent they move from one type of culture to another (see, for example, Graves (1981)). It is also a powerful tool for analyzing the need for organization change when market conditions change, and shows how

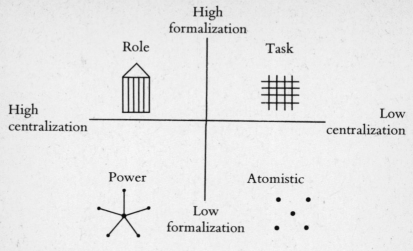

Figure 2.1   *Harrison's four culture types*

changes made across the model (e.g. from 'power' to 'task') will create much more organizational upheaval than changes round the model (e.g. from 'power' to 'role'). (See Figure 2.1.)

Despite its theoretical weakness, the model has interesting parallels. For instance, the basic Jungian concepts of introversion/extroversion and judgement/perception may be used to construe different managerial types. Those who are judgemental will adapt well to a centralized organization. Similarly, those who are intuitive may need the freedom of task-type or atomistic cultures, whereas those who learn from their senses may prefer the more robust type of power culture.

In her study of Jungian types, Myers (1962) demonstrated that business students had significantly different profiles from scientists and engineers. For the first group, extroversion, learning cognitively ('sensing') and processing analytically ('thinking') were characteristic: the second and third groups tended to learn more intuitively and the engineers tended to be more judgemental and less perceptive in their approach to problems. Both tended towards introversion.

A study by Kleiner (1983) covering 437 organization members supports these views. He found that in America, extroverted, sensing, thinking and judging types outnumbered introverted, intuitive, feeling/perceiving types by about three to two (p. 1009). Furthermore, he found that the former preferred to work in organizations characterized by high task-activity and high formality of structure because such organizations appeared to provide meaningful assistance in enhancing their reported quality of working life, with motivation, work satisfaction and quality of life (p.1007). It therefore follows that each major category of personality (ESTJ, ISTJ, INTJ) will seek a culture where it is happiest. These cultures may be what Harrison describes as the power, role and task cultures respectively.

Mention of learning leads to consideration of the work of Kolb (1976). He suposed that people learn in four different ways:

(1) By active experimentation.
(2) By concrete experience.
(3) By reflective observation.
(4) By abstract conceptualization.

Harrison's insight is enriched by the substitution of these four methods for the term 'centralization' and 'formalization' as in Figure 2.2.

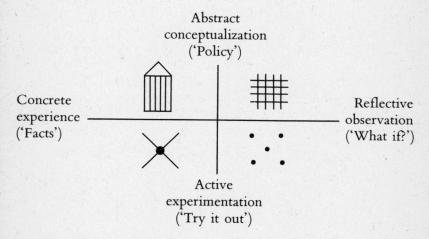

Figure 2.2 *Kolb learning styles applied to Harrison grid*

Kolb's contention was that learning starts with one of the four activities and proceeds (either clockwise or counter-clockwise) with each other activity. He also stated (and this borne out by Stamp (1981)) that managers tended to become fixated in one mode. Furthermore, different styles were used in different occupations, a salesman using active experimentation or concrete experience while a research officer would use abstract conceptualization and reflective observation. These findings are borne out by experience, since sales offices are created in the power mode, while laboratories use a matrix quite frequently. Thus Wales (1980) and others see learning theory (either Jungian or Kolbian) as underpinning the Harrison model.

There is another respect in which Harrison's four-culture model may be the result of the way the whole subject of comparative organization study has been handled. Heydebrand (1973) has isolated twenty-three organizational variables used to compare organizations. These range from size to effectiveness. In a summary of and commentary on the literature in this field, Kostecki and Mrela (1983) have pointed out that these variables resolve into three dimensons:

(1) *Extent of contextualisation*
    The degree to which the environments of organizations are compared.
(2) *Structuring of roles versus structuring of performance*
    The degree to which the shape of the organization is more important than its outputs.
(3) *Administrative complexity versus technological complexity*
    The degree to which complexity is seen as an administrative rather than a technical phenomenon.

Using the Harrison categorization it might be inferred that each 'culture' represented a partiality of description. For example, descriptions of a role culture organization would concentrate upon the structuring of roles and administrative complexity and the relative unimportance of context, as if only these elements were crucial to an understanding of organizations. The fact that people see their organizations as role cultures would imply a focusing of interest upon certain aspects of organizational life and a screening out of other aspects. In this case the tendency may be for students of comparative organization to see what they describe because it is impossible to describe what they see. In this case we should beware of attempting to classify organizations according to Harrison's four cultures because they are four descriptions of the same phenomenon. However, the fact that organization populations differ significantly from one another in psychological terms enables us to distinguish perceptions, although not categorize realities. Thus any propositions about these cultures must surely be interpreted to mean 'the organization *is seen as*' rather than 'the organization *is*' since, as Kostecki and Mrela point out, 'it is impossible to ascertain which similarities/dissimilarities between organizations are artefacts of research tools and research design, and which are reflections of reality' (p.85).

In a valiant attempt to map the various components into a comparative management model, Tung (1978) suggested consideration of many variables. Her model embraced:

(i)   Societal environment variables, e.g. economic, political.
(ii) Organizational environment variables, e.g. technology, structure and processes.
(iii) Personal variables, including members' perception of organizational culture.
(iv) Outcome variables, mainly job satisfaction and economic measures of effectiveness.

The interesting part of her schema was the attempt to create systematic relationships. While she accepted that the four main variables are interdependent, she argued that members' perception of organizational culture is influenced by organizational process, job satisfaction, effectiveness of the organization, motivation and personal attributes. She argued that perceptions also affect organizational processes so the culture and processes would appear to be mutually reinforcing. She suggested that comparative management involves 'the examination of bi-directional relationships, simultaneous investigation of organizational and psychological processes and investigation of feedback circuits that exist between different sets of variables' (p.295). While this extends well into the realms of meta-research, it is important to note the salience given in this model to personal attributes.

Summary and conclusions

This brief review of the literature indicates that previous thinkers and researchers have adopted one of three viewpoints concerning culture:

(1) The culture is a product of the context — the market in which the organization operates, the legal constraints, and so on. (Payne and Pugh (1976)).

(2) The culture is a product of the structures and functions to be found within the organization. A centralized organization will have a different culture from a decentralized one, for example. (Harrison (1972)).

(3) The culture is a product of people's attitudes to their work: it is the product of the individual psychological contracts with the organization. (James and Jones (1974)).

Each of these separate approaches has at some time been combined with each of the others.

Each approach, however, suffers from the disadvantage that it treats culture as objective, as if everyone in the world would be able to observe the same phenomenon, whereas this is patently not the case. 'Outsiders' do not have the same sense of culture as 'insiders'. It therefore becomes necessary to look for another explanation.

Schneider and Reichers (1983) have come to the same conclusion as the author: that culture is commonly perceived because the psychological sets of the actors are themselves common. They pointed out that individuals are attracted to jobs and organizations which fit their personalities (Holland, (1973)) in which they can implement their self-concepts (Super, (1953)) and from which they can obtain outcomes they desire, particularly need satisfactions (Vroom, (1964); Wanous, (1980)). Thus individuals are engaged in a process of self-selection as they decide which organizations to approach for employment.

Organizations, on the other hand, frequently marshal considerable amounts of resources in order to attract 'right types' — people whose attitudes, values, goals and job performance will be consistent with the organization's expectations. This is precisely the purpose for all forms of recruitment and selection in which organizations engage. [Schneider and Reichers (1983), p. 27]

Wilkins has made the same point.

It has already been noted that organizations frequently go to lengths to attract the 'right type' (Silverman and Jones) so we may proceed legitimately to investigate culture by means of an instrument that measures traits. However, one problem has to be overcome — that of climates. We address this in two ways. First, the research on climate tends to use discrete work groups. Secondly, the researchers operate at a low level. Gerwin (1979) and Gregory (1983) have both emphasized the importance of what the latter calls the 'native-view paradigm'. In the research to be recounted in the next chapters, the members of the main sub-samples were all representative of senior levels of management, chosen for their eligibility for general management. In order to be so chosen it is likely that they reflect, at least in the eyes of their superiors or the personnel department, the total culture of the organization such that they are able to work effectively within it. Furthermore, the use of the character traits of organization members to distinguish between organizations does not necessarily mean that different sub-groups may not have different climates. As has previously been shown, the term 'culture' is a general and pervasive guide, not a meticulous rule-book. So, as Schneider and Reichers conclude:

While consistency in organizational structure and similarities among organization members may combine to diminish individual differences and produce organizational climates, work group climates within the same organization vary as a function of intense interaction patterns within groups as compared to across groups. [p.33]

This is a clear example of the muddle that could be avoided were different words to be used — we have suggested organizational *culture* and work group *climate*.

In particular, the studies so far reviewed cover

— the external influences on climate (e.g. Payne and Pugh).
— the internally perceived climate (e.g. the Michigan studies).

— the psychological climate (e.g. James and Jones).
— the behavioural climate (e.g. Litwin and Stringer).

Personality is seen only as a moderating factor between organizational culture and psychological climate. In a recent review of the literature, Field and Abelson (1982), quoting with approval the James and Jones' creation of the concept of psychological climate, proposed that it be given more attention and promoted it to being the central concept, linked directly to the environmental influences and moderated, as before, by personality. In their recommendations for further research they laid stress upon five areas:

(i)   They look for greater differentiation between organization, group and psychological climate.

(ii) Research should view *psychological climate* (and not organizational climate) *as being the most central of the three types of climate.* Climate is a perceptual interpretation of the environment and each person has their own perception. Organizational and group climate occur when there is a consensus among many individual perceptions within the particular unit under analysis. [p.197.] But where do these perceptions spring from? The psychologist would argue that it is personality that conditions these perceptions.

(iii) A single climate instrument which would be valid across organizations should be developed. This is easier to say than do because, as can easily be imagined, the number of possible creators of climate is vast, and not limited only to the four elements identified by the Michigan school as Autonomy, Degree of Structure, Rewards and Consideration–Warmth–Support. The only climate instrument that can easily be applied is a tool to measure the modal personality of those employed in the focal part of the organization — those responsible for disseminating the culture.

(iv) They also look for more climate research which utilizes experimental design and longitudinal field studies. Certainly research using experimental designs has not been much reported. The problem with these is that one is obliged to specify *a priori* the climates to be measured; and this limits the concept. As for longitudinal field studies, they are unlikely to provide much of value since the climate does not remain unchanged for long, because the independent variables such as leadership, structure and market dependence are in constant process of change.

(v) They propose a moratorium on arguments as to whether the climate construct exists. However, nothing in the literature has been able to measure it, still less define it, and even if it is accepted that psychological climate exists, we are still reduced to a Thomasian approach to climate as the subjective expression of a felt need, rather than the objective statement of a phenomenon.

What follows, then, is in part a verification of their main suggestion — the discovery of culture through the character of the people in the organization, together with some speculation as to the reasons for the differences between organizations. What will still be lacking is an explanation of how this climate is created, and this is beyond the scope of this book. For the determined scholar we have included in the Appendix a review of the literature by which some of our thinking has been affected.

3 Going through the hoop

Introduction

If it is true that you can understand a man by the company he keeps, then a good way to understand a company is by the people it keeps. You might measure the way groups of people from different companies react to the same stimulus — if the reactions were observably different it would be possible to classify the groups. Stimuli might be of any sort: problems requiring the use of initiative, intelligence, ingenuity or determination — all qualities said to be valuable for the conduct of business. At another level one might evaluate the attitudes of people towards the administration of such tests: enjoyment of the challenge, resentment of the competitive situation, indifference to the outcome and so forth. At another level still, one might obtain information about the differing value systems of the groups in the sense of their belief in the efficacy of stimuli as an aid to understanding, willingness to trust experts and confidence in the validity of the conclusions. Thus, a set of carefully chosen stimuli might provide the beginning of a codification of behaviour, attitudes and beliefs — the culture — of an organization. However, not all levels of the organization are equally affected by culture: at the lower levels it is the rule book which dominates, and people move from one company to another unaffected by changes in culture. It is only at the senior levels that culture plays an important part in corporate activity — the level where 'company politics' becomes a factor to be reckoned with in daily business life. So, in measuring culture we would look, for preference, at those whose job is the maintenance of discipline and the motivation to achieve corporate goals.

A golden opportunity to do this occurs at management training establishments where groups of senior managers undergo extended programmes of management development designed to improve both their individual skills and their understanding of how their organization operates in its environment. From the moment an organization decides to carry out senior level training a complex chain of interaction is unleashed which provides a rich fund of information about the company: its values about making managers 'go through hoops'; its attitudes to the training establishment and its behaviour before, during and after the programme has been run. The author was fortunate to work at the Oxford Centre for Management Studies for nine years, during which time he was involved in the setting up and direction of programmes commissioned by organizations for their own employees. These programmes ran for many years consecutively. During that time he noticed many of the differences referred to and came to appreciate that some of the reasons for the differences arose from the differing cultures. He quickly became aware of the need to treat the clients and their employees differently despite the fact that they all said they wanted to same thing — management training. Even the treatment of the material to be taught had to be varied to suit the culture, for while the managers being trained were at the Centre (now renamed Templeton College) it became a part of the culture. The Oxford Management Centre is peculiarly sensitive to this, as it was designed and built to accommodate relatively small groups of managers and is only able to cater for two or three such groups at a time, so the influence of the corporate culture was particularly strongly felt. What follows is the description of the origins and operation of courses for four organizations covering their genesis; the design of the first programme and subsequent adaptations; monitoring and evaluation; and an assessment of the possible effects of the training upon the organization. The companies are: a retail chain store group; a local government agency; a manufacturing organization and an insurance broking organization. We shall see what hoops were used, and of what size, and the criteria for a successful jump; we are not concerned here with the organizations as entities, but only with the way they reacted to an external stimulus.

Senior management development in a retail chain store group

Over a period of fifteen years this group developed a special relationship with the Centre, which represents the closest example of an off-site training wing. In interviews with two directors who had been involved in setting up the course the Centre was referred to as 'a sheet-anchor', 'an institution', 'a management development centre, not just a place for training'.

The contact originated with an approach in 1967 from the director of the newly-formed Centre to the (non-executive) chairman of the Group, who agreed to send one person (a director-designate) on a six month long training course. As a result, the Group's Board decided to embark upon a programme of training for senior stores and buying management, to compensate for a perceived dearth of promotable managers. Directors were invited to make nominations which were then vetted by the personnel director and his manager. In the end, ten men were selected (the first female came in 1973) of which seven came from store management. The objective was to give training to senior executives 'with potential for future development or who required training to improve their performance'.

The programme was designed jointly by members of the personnel department and Fellows of the Centre. It was not intended to be too academic since the participants had, in the main, no tertiary education: many had left school at sixteen. All members were briefed beforehand and debriefed afterwards. The course was monitored in the usual way and the managing director attended the final session. At the one-day debriefing participants were invited to make suggestions for changes and many were, in fact, made, particularly in the marketing and human relations areas.

Both during the course and afterwards the emphasis was upon challenge: nothing was learnt without rigorous testing — just as in the business. It quickly became apparent, however, that the main benefit (according to the directors interviewed) came from 'the interaction of the participants themselves'.

The three directors interviewed during the research were not unanimous in their assessment of the effect upon the culture of management development. The senior one thought it had little direct effect on the culture. His former assistant thought that it had been critical to the development of the business because it had created an ability among participants to 'look at things in a corporate sense and had given people a better sense of proportion — management development is an accepted part of our culture. Management development does not change the business but it emphasizes the change in the philosophy or culture of the business.' The third director was more cautious: 'It broadens the men's understanding of commerce and benefits also the people to whom they return — over the long term it improves the quality of management, although this is not easy to quantify.'

It is easy to dismiss such subjective judgements by three senior officers of a retail group as so much self-justification. There are, however, a number of interesting features about the Group's experience. First, there is the enthusiasm for training *per se*. For a business that thrives upon statistics, it is surpising to find support for the unquantifiable effects of training. Second, there is the sense of personal involvement. None of the three directors had actually been on the course (although one had been on another six-month course at the Centre), but they took the trouble, each year, to brief the Fellows on the personal characteristics, needs and qualities of the participants. Third, there was the projection onto the Centre of hopes for the well-being of the business itself. The Centre was seen as 'a sheet-anchor' and the sessions attended by directors were always used to air grievances and explain faults in policy as well as providing an occasion for announcing good news. Finally, there is the spirit of challenge. At the pre-course briefing the implication conveyed by the personnel department was that the course was some kind of test that might only be survived with great effort. In summary, the corporate culture is reflected in the directness of approach to the business of development training and the emphasis upon challenge.

Management development in a local government agency

The decision to undertake management training was taken at a Council meting in June 1972. The Director of Establishments put

up a request for the Council to become Corporate Members of the
Centre

> to enable the Council to take advantage of the facilities provided
> by the Centre, particularly for the training and development of
> senior officers and those with the potential to succeed to those
> positions. The needs of these officers for training and development
> are rather special and cannot adequately be dealt with by our in-
> service training programme or our normal use of business schools
> and staff colleges which are more appropriate to more junior
> officers.

The laconic request with its rather arrogant overtones was the
outcome of a series of coincidences and was nearly to prove
disastrous.

After a number of meetings with the personnel subcommittee of
the Chief Officer's Board (one of whom happened to be the chief
architect, who liked the unusual style of the Centre's building), it was
decided to run a trial course; its objectives (the result of copious re-
drafting by five levels of officer within the personnel department)
were stated as:

> To achieve a better understanding of
>
> (a) the decision-making processes in the Council and the ways in
>   which they could be aided both at organization and individual
>   levels; and
> (b) the effect on the role of and decision-making in the Council
>   of environmental factors, particularly its relationship with
>   central and local government and with the economic and
>   political and social environment as a whole.

The reason for such an elaborately worded objective was the intention
of the Council to test (even to destruction!) the capability of the
Centre to handle senior officers. After some discussions as to the
programme, twelve senior men were nominated from the succession
charts. They included six who were shortly to become Chief
Officers. Partly as a defensive measure, and partly out of ignorance

of the field, the writer planned a course with forty-seven classroom sessions of one and a half hours each (in just under ten working days) with twenty-four speakers.

As might be expected, the course was something of a fiasco. Each speaker was quickly appraised, criticized and demolished: only the breaks provided some light relief. It was seen to have failed to achieve its objective, to be weak in programme content and instruction and to provide no basis for continuing self-development. Only the administration and accommodation were satisfactory. The evaluations were written out in great detail and contained such helpful comments as the following:

On Standard of Instruction
The general standard of external speakers was high, but that of some College staff was poor ... The lecturer on Local Government Finance and other matters had a well-worn set of notes he must have used many times before but apparently had not consulted recently.

On the Advantage of Using OCMS
I have concluded that the level of knowledge, expertise and experience displayed by the Fellows of the Centre and other contributors to the course is easily matched by a cross section of local government officers of a comparable age and responsibility level.

On the Relevance of the Course for Future Development
I learnt very little of any practical use . . . I got more value out of a two-day crash course in rapid reading.

The participants were unanimous about the inability of the Centre to cater for the needs of local government and only one member suggested that the course was a good 'first approximation'. Given the comments quoted above, one might reasonably expect the course to founder: the fact that it has run regularly each year ever since is as good an indication as any of the nature of the Council's culture.

In the first place, they were sensitive to the goodwill generated by the Centre. Immediately after the evaluations had been received, the Liaison Fellow was invited to visit each participant to seek guidance upon possible improvements: the greatest help was given by the person who had been rudest about the programme.

Secondly, having committed itself to a course of action, the Department seemed unwilling to cut its losses without a further experiment. In the meantime, the political complexion of the Council had swung from blue to pink but the new administration did not seem reluctant to continue the experiment. Accordingly, a one-day briefing seminar was organized at the Centre, chaired jointly by the Chief Executive and the Chairman of the Personnel Committee, in order to give Fellows a nodding acquaintance with the structure, aims and operations of the Council. The course was then redesigned with less ambitious objectives, although still in the decision-making area, and with more Council speakers. The Council also reduced the level of participant somewhat (only three have so far become Chief Officers). The level was still high enough to have destroyed the course had they wished, but again coincidence played a part — this time in respect of the tone of the group which was much more supportive and in respect of a heavy input on the subject of planning and budgeting in local government, including a case study from a Canadian expert who happened to be a friend of the director of the Centre.

Additionally, some important facts about local government officers' learning styles had been acquired:

(1) they were capable of coping with vast quantities of material which they could absorb superficially without enquiring very deeply into it. It therefore became necessary to vastly increase the quantity (but not necessarily the quality) of input;

(2) they were impressed by status — at least initially. A poor speaker of high status was more readily listened to than a good speaker of low status;

(3) they were eager to take part in group activities providing these did not have decisions as their output;

(4) they were always willing to express views on any issue.

All these behaviours arise, as will be appreciated, from the nature of bureaucratic work with its (outward, at any rate) respect for authority, its mountains of paperwork, its endless committees and its oral and voluntary selection procedure, involving questions and answers.

As soon as it became plain that decision-making was not something that local government officers did, the subject of the course changed. Both the subject and the format were therefore changed each year to suit the current needs of the service. For administrative reasons, the 1974 course was run in early 1975 when the interest had switched to the world economic crisis and topics that had been praised previously were now considered irrelevant. A particular instance was the case of local government planning and budgeting: the system was now established in the Council and therefore of no further interest! The course had been extended into Saturday of the middle weekend giving a total of fifty-eight sessions, of which thirty-one were now handled by local government experts, and only eight by Fellows of the Centre: this displeased the Centre and justified the pompous remarks about the first course.

The participants began to be interested in giving some feedback to the Council, and by the fourth programme, in late 1975, had started the practice of sending resumés of their project presentations to County Hall with the request that they be considered. This reached its apogee in 1978 when the Chief Executive and his Heads of Personnel and Finance sat for an afternoon to listen to them. However, they had little impact upon management thinking and, despite the quality of the work that was put into them, were eventually abandoned.

By 1976, the course had become 'fashionable' within the Council. Officers sought to be nominated as a means to further promotion, or at least a method of widening their personal contact network and understanding of the Council as an entity (an intellectual legerdemain only made possible at the course by the combination of a wide spread of departmental provenance — twelve representatives of twelve different departments — and senior level of speaker). For the first time the leaders of both parties deemed it worth their while to be present, as did the most senior of the officers. Unusually, for courses of this kind, the quality of participant remained constant (due, perhaps, to the large size of the organization). Two members of the 1976 course have since become Chief Officers. The participants now began to be more interested in the outside world: accordingly, more time was given to subjects not directly connected with the working of the council such as economics and the social environment.

When the courses had been running for five years the Council decided to invite all the participants to a seminar at which the whole question of performance was debated. Under the title of 'The Main Issues Facing the Council Over the Next Five Years', another paper was submitted to the Chief Executive highlighting the problems of 'roles and relationships, particularly those between members and officers, and their impact on effective performance'. It suggested that working relationships between officers and between departments had improved markedly — and that the courses had significantly contributed to this improvement, and went on to advocate a conference at the Centre to advance the matter further. The seminar, which was attended by forty-five of the original fifty-five participants, proved that after a fortnight at the Centre, participants were able to work together effectively in mixed groups without the normal 'warming-up' period. This, at least, they had learnt from attendance at the courses.

Typically, once a bureaucracy has internalized something like a management development activity, it does not easily discard it even when it may no longer be regarded as relevant and the standard of senior officer has fallen below the level envisaged in the original submission. The programmes remain memorable, not so much for the learning that took place (although there were some brilliant debates) nor even for the humorous moments but most of all for the personalities of the individuals. It is a truism that in bureaucracies things only get done by people who can work through the interstices of the carapace, and the Council was no exception. Participants had risen to high office in the service by being able to 'play the system' as well as being substantial people in their own right — humane supervisors and indefatigable servants of a system that appeared to be almost impossible to operate. They all seemed better managers than their counterparts in the private sector, not least because they had less power over their subordinates.

Training manufacturing managers

The history of the manufacturing company's involvement with the Centre is essentially the history of one training cycle and one assignment for a senior manager in management development. Although training itself was normally carried out by highly professional insiders (and in some instances outsiders) the job of organizing and presenting the programmes was assigned to a career marketing man transferred into management development for a short period. Thus, in this case the liaison man in the company learnt to train whilst organizing the training; his success and promotion was dependent upon the success of the programme as a whole.

The training cycle itself arose out of reports based on employee surveys that the organization was becoming too task-orientated and that this was reducing morale. As one director put it: 'management consists of plugging the gap between targets and achievements', the usual method being high rewards. He conceded, however, that the degree of mutual criticism within the company was apt to be time-wasting. In other words, the system of management emphasized control rather than consideration and it was the task of the training cycle to redress the balance.

The first approach of the manager was to hire space in training centres and put on his own courses: the idea of using non-company trainers was not, at first, too popular. Then, reasoning that the message might be somewhat more convincing coming from outsiders, he decided to take the risk of employing speakers from the Centre. To do this, he and his professional associates made a presentation to the Fellows backed up with detailed documentation.

There then ensued a lengthy planning process involving the design, implementation and timing of the programme to the nearest minute.

The first two programmes were then run (in September and November 1977), and found to be only moderately successful, due to the lack of knowledge about the company on the part of non-company speakers and lack of relevent teaching material. It is usual for these criticisms to be made of non-company speakers, and the problem can be overcome by intellectual efort on the part of the audience.

But this was not good enough for the company. The manager having decided that the concept was relevant, resolved to create his own materials and, with the help of the Centre, devised a set of role-plays and critical incidents based upon his own experiences that would make the points that had failed to come across using non-company materials. He achieved such proficiency at this that by the time the cycle ended (i.e. all the relevant personnel had received the training) he had devised series of teaching aids and a whole-day case study. In constructing the incidents he was assisted by various professional trainers, but he himself wrote the final draft and in the classroom played the role of the person under consideration.

The content of these 'scenes from daily life' are of interest. They bear mainly upon internal conflict ('people spend more time selling within than selling to customers' he once said), and the effect of the company upon the individual.

Examples of the first kind were: arguments about internal transfers; failure to achieve targets; failure of managers to effectively manage their subordinates; failure of an individual to treat a junior employee with respect. Examples of the second kind were: a wife ringing her husband's boss to complain about the effect of excessive job pressure on the marriage; people leaving the organization to work for a competitor firm started by an ex-employee (unacceptable!) or of a family business (marginally acceptable but wasteful!); and (the long case study) a malingerer running a private business (he was actually sacked, then reinstated!) All these cases were based upon the manager's own experience.

In addition to revising the material, consideration was given to the quality of the trainers, and in the guise of asking for demonstrations of how to train, the outside trainers were given feedback and advice on the improvement of their techniques.

Eventually, by the time the next phase of courses was run, the design and content of the programme (if not the message) had been considerably modified, and as the trainers modified their style so as to become increasingly provocative, slick and humorous, the training manager was able to observe the participants' satisfaction with the courses rise considerably. These examples hopefully give the tone of the general training cycle.

Similar training was given to these managers' bosses but here the accent was different. Some of these men had reached their ceiling and were reflecting whether the effort had been worthwhile, while others were looking forward (somewhat apprehensively) to further promotion. The outcome of such discussions would usually be a recognition of the sense of isolation of the senior manager — out of the mainstream of reward-linked effort, but insufficiently equipped to deal with the human problems of managing without powers of carrot and stick. With such a high premium on success, the problems of failure are internalized to a much greater extent than in other less achievement-based companies. Paradoxically, it appears that while success is bought from the individual by the company, and leaves his ownership, failure stays with him. The system wins and the individual loses.

The culmination of the cycle was the involvement of the board of directors in a version of the course, compressed into one working day:

(1) To provide executive management with feedback from Management Programmes:
   — messages from subordinates
   — observations from trainees
(2) To provide the opportunity for executive management to debate some of the key issues raised by the programme.
(3) To discuss the ongoing development programme and seek the continuing support of executive Management.

The programme consisted partly of talks, partly of exercises and partly of discussion. Due to the careful preparation which is the hallmark of the management development activity within the company, it ran to time and generated profitable discussion. The board, far from feeling threatened by their 'exposure' as poor appraisers and only moderately good managers, was able to obtain considerable insights from the data presented.

In the one-day seminar, the executive management was told that although managers were good at communicating they were less effective at developing their subordinates' skills, at acknowledging and discussing performance, and at considering their needs as individuals.

This account calls for a number of comments. The first is that in training as in everything else, this company tries harder to do a good job than most other companies. Second, their executives carry the apparent respect for the individual to great lengths. They were individually most agreeable to work with. In their solutions to role-plays the managers were probably more authoritarian in the classroom than they would be in real life. Third, the training manager was concerned to have favourable feedback from his trainees to pass on.

Training in an insurance broking company

The concept of management development arose out of the managing director's wish to improve the general standard of management in his firm. From the early discussions he had been aware of the shortage of good administrators capable of taking on senior responsibility in the company, and one of the objectives of the training programme was to rectify this.

After some discussion with the contact Fellow (in this case, the writer), an in-depth approach to the problem was devised. First, a week's training would be given to the top management of the UK division. This would be followed later in the month by a strategy seminar for the top management of the firm (excluding the chairman, directors and company secretary, who were considered to be part of the holding company), and then two days would be spent planning the course. The first two events were planned and steered by Fellows of the Centre and proceeded normally. The third event was not planned in any formal sense. The company sent twelve middle managers of the type that would be attending the courses and they were asked to specify first, the training needs, then the methods, and finally the duration and time-table for the courses. This two-day event was attended by the group administration director (a non-specialist) and the newly-appointed personnel director.

There was, as may be imagined, a certain amount of suspicion and hostility on the part of those who had been sent. Most of them had not been on a training course before and were not clear about the purpose of the two days. However, by the end of the period sufficient consensus had been achieved to enable a course to be planned, in which, as they said:

— there would be an opportunity to see whether we have any teeth when the managing director comes

— the lack of trust in the personnel department would be broken down
— the course would not be an exercise in brainwashing
— 'people' subjects (e.g. motivation, selection, delegation) would occupy much of the time
— the corporate strategy would be explained

In the end the subjects chosen included communication, basic accounts, marketing, management of time, decision-making, and, in general, the behavioural skills that tend to be overlooked in management teaching. The programme that emerged was more 'down to earth' than the Centre would have planned it, and had the merit of approximately satisfying the perceived needs of the group.

Also present at all three sessions was the recently retired managing director of the UK group. After a career in selling insurance, he was requested by the managing director to act as the company's liaison man and organizer — in addition to the newly-appointed personnel director. His presence, experience and seniority were, at first, an inhibiting factor upon the group, but as the series continued he was invaluable in ensuring continuity, and the fact that he was no longer part of the organization lent weight to his interventions.

The details of the first courses were now elaborated, with active assistance from the personnel director who wished to be identified with the project. The purpose of the courses was defined as:

(i)   To develop further management understanding and skills.
(ii)   To participate in an up-to-date review and discussion of group operations, performance and plans.

The content, developed on the advice of Directors and Senior Managers in the Group, will include:

(i)   Group organisation and business strategy.
(ii)   Principles of management — planning forecasting, goal-setting, organising, etc.
(iii) Managing skills.
(iv)   Legislation affecting staff relations.
(v)   Project work on current company issues.

This quotation, from the letter sent out to senior directors with a request for nominations to the first two courses, indicates a rather high level of expectations for a mere two-week programme. The first programme, duly run as advertised, was attended by three of the original planning group, and nine others of equal or greater seniority (all members of the original group attended as availability permitted). The course ran right through the middle weekend and some time was spent on syndicate work leading up to presentations on three previously nominated topics.

The evaluations of the first two courses were enthusiastic, and the objectives were said to be achieved. Three points of interest arose in respect of the first course: first, several participants stated specifically that they preferred outsider speakers to company speakers — who might be 'biased'; second, the syndicate projects were seen to 'show the worth of the whole course and should certainly be maintained'; they were later scrapped because of the third criticism, namely, that there was insufficient time to cover the topics in depth.

The evaluation of the second course was similar, except that by now the participants were beginning to be aware of the value of company speakers (where these were relatively recent recruits and so not too 'company-minded'), and most people were asking that their bosses should be sent. The top men had already been to the one-week programme in June the previous year, but the remark perhaps applies generally rather than to particular people and is a not uncommon reaction at middle management level.

The course now settled down into a long run. Not all the courses were given at the Centre, but Centre teachers were used at other sites, in order to maintain uniformity, because a suspicion was aroused that non-Oxford courses were somehow inferior to Oxford-based courses. Non-Oxford speakers were also used both at Oxford and elsewhere. The projects were replaced by a two-day interactive computerized business game and weekend working was abandoned. However, the continuity was maintained by the retired senior manager who sat through almost every session and endowed it with what he thought would be the company character — humorous and challenging, but not too radical.

Over the years, as well as strategy seminars, special courses were run, including specially designed programmes for the men's direct bosses and for the administration managers and for the managements of individual parts of the group. In 1981 it was decided to ask the 167 people who had attended the course in the four years of its life to evaluate it. By this time, twenty-four had left or were unavailable, so 143 questionnaires were sent out, and 94 returned (62.9 per cent). The majority selected 'people' subjects as those which had most helped in the job. However, they now were most eager to learn about finance and accounting (perhaps a reflection of their increased responsibilities). Sixty-one per cent of the respondents had taken part in a project, either during or after the course (one project was to write the script for an in-house film that was made about management training; another was to design a follow-up programme for the more successful of those who had been on the initial programme) and virtually all had found it useful. Finally, when asked to select from a list the benefits of the course, the following items were most popular:

(1) 'Having time to think' was placed first by 36.6 per cent of participants
(2) 'Meeting other people' was placed first by 26.6 per cent of participants
(3) 'Learning new techniques' was placed first by 24.4 per cent of participants

All these topics were also the *second* choice of 21.2 per cent of participants, as was the topic 'obtaining a broader view of the company'. This latter topic was also the *third* choice of 25.5 per cent of the participants, which seems to indicate that people are interested in themselves first and the company second. This view is supported by the fact that 'learning about company policies' was the most frequent *fourth* choice (29 per cent) and both were jointly preferred *fifth* choice. Table 3.1 shows the percentages.

They were also asked to list ways in which they had changed since attending the course. The most frequently mentioned change was an improvement (subjectively assessed!) in handling subordinates, followed by improvement in self-assurance and understanding of business techniques (the 'principles of management'!).

Some attempt was made to discover which topics had caused the change (although this question was not specifically asked), by

Table 3.1 *The benefits of the course in order of merit*

Benefit of course	Ranking (% of participants)				
	1	2	3	4	5
Having time to think	36.6	21.1	13.3	6.6	6.6
Meeting other people	26.6	21.1	18.8	12.2	13.3
Learning new techniques	24.9	21.1	10.0	16.6	13.3
Matching yourself against others	3.3	5.5	11.1	13.3	11.1
Obtaining a broader view of the company	7.7	21.1	25.5	17.7	16.6
Learning about company policies	0	6.6	16.6	20.0	16.6
Meeting senior members of the company	1	4.4	5.5	6.6	12.2

equating cases where two-thirds of all respondents mentioning a topic also mentioned an improvement in a particular area. The improvement in handling subordinates does not derive from one particular subject (all are mentioned) but mainly from human skills and decision-making. Increase in self-confidence arises mainly from better understanding of economics and decision-making, and better skills at interviewing and public speaking.

By 1982 it was possible to begin running the advanced courses mentioned above: these were more issue-based than topic-based and run for only one week.

Conclusions

It will be seen from Table 3.2 that the four companies in the sub-sample do differ quite markedly in their approach to training, and this may reflect differences in the value system of the company. At least it is possible to demonstrate differences in one important sphere of management activity which might not seem explicable by chance. It will be seen that training is handled quite differently if it represents a departure from previous practice or is a new routine, if the company is interested in training itself or simply using it as a social device.

Table 3.2 *Comparison of training approaches*

Stage of operation	Retailing group	Local government agency	Manufacturing organization	Insurance broker
Initial contact	Board	Personal contact	Chief Executive	MD
Authority given by	Board	Council	Training Director	MD
Design of first programme	Board committee	Personnel officer	Management development manager	Managers themselves
Individual pre-course briefing	Half-day	None	None	None
Initial monitoring and evaluation	Meeting with Fellows	Written and verbal, designed by Council	Session by session	Designed by Centre
Personnel director's involvement	High	Minimal	Minimal	High when appointed
Subsequent alterations to programme	Minor	Annual re-vamp	Minor	Minor
Current status	Continues	End of cycle	Continues	Continues
Effects of training	'Improvement of understanding'	'Greater corporate spirit'	Feedback to management	Uncertain

In retrospect, it becomes apparent that training is used for all sorts of political purposes, and the mutual attempts of top management and participants to influence one another's activities through the training medium is an under-researched area, as is the role of the training manager in subverting or changing the culture.

It will be seen from the table that in certain cases the chief executive was intimately involved in the start-up and continuation of the courses (all of them attended the courses to preside over question and answer sessions). Some of the reasons have already been alluded to (e.g. political). In all cases, however, the characters and desires of the chief executives were reflected in the type and method of training adopted.

4. Diagnosing the culture

Introduction

One of the crucial questions concerning corporate culture may be stated as follows: if it is true that organization cultures exist and can be identified, do these cultures arise from character traits of the employees, or from the way in which they accept norms of behaviour imposed by an external stimulus? It might be that the general population of senior managers (the 'high priests' of the organization's culture) are a homogeneous group of experts in culture transmission (among other things). Or it may be that senior managers are promoted to high positions in their particular organizations because of special character or personality traits that earmark them as symbols of the organization culture. An example of the corporate recognition of this state of affairs might be companies where the head of a functional department is a generalist and not a specialist (e.g. personnel and estates departments in banks). This would reinforce Bate's (1984) view of the significance of the decision-making system for the maintenance of the culture.

An opportunity arose to test this proposition, using the Ghiselli Self-Description Inventory, in the four companies described in Chapter Three. In what follows these sub-samples will be analyzed and compared with a control sample of 612 managers. First, the general characteristics of the total sample will be described and compared with those of the four sub-samples. Then the sample and sub-samples will be submitted to two techniques of analysis — discriminant analysis, which computes the likelihood of significant differences occurring between the sub-samples, and factor analysis, which endeavours to elicit the special characteristics of groups of people in the sample and sub-samples. It will be shown that the same factors are present in the sample and in the sub-samples but that they occur in a different order. It will also be shown that the sub-samples can be discriminated statistically and along three main dimensions which form the basis of a taxonomy of organization 'collective-character' traits.

General description of sample and sub-samples

The total sample consisted of 612 senior managers who attended general management training programmes at the Management Centre between 1979 and 1983. Apart from fifty-four people attending a public course for senior managers, the programmes were all of the in-house, off-site training type described in the previous chapter. The following sub-samples were used:

Chain store — seventy-four managers
Local government agency — seventy-four senior managers
Manufacturing company — forty-three senior managers and directors of the main board
Insurance broker — 101 senior managers and directors of the chief subsidiaries.

All these managers were either directors, or within one or two levels of the main board.

Selection of research tool

Self-report questionnaires may produce data that is satisfying for the user, but are not necessarily valid as an instrument for research. The writer has, therefore, chosen an instrument that was not easy to falsify, because it operated on the basis of statistical inference rather than self-description. Furthermore, the tool had to be easy to administer and quick to mark, so that feedback could be given to managers during their stay at the Centre. Finally, the test had to be one that gave reliable information about managers, as distinct from other members of the population. Fineman (1975) indicated that in his opinion the Ghiselli inventory combined these desiderata better than twenty-one other published tests for measuring achievement motivation. After experimenting with other questionnaires, such as the Bales (1970) value questionnaire, the Myers Briggs indicator, and the Harrison questionnaire, the Ghiselli tool was selected as the best approximation to what was needed.

Table 4.1 *Ghiselli's estimate of correlates with job success*

Trait	Correlation with job success
Self-assurance	+ .19
Decisiveness	+ .22
Supervisory ability	+ .46
Intelligence	+ .27
Initiative	+ .15
Need for achievement	+ .34
Need for self-actualization	+ .26
Need for power	+ .03
Need for reward	− .18
Need for security	− .30

In his research Ghiselli (1971) set out to test some of the trait theories of management, to see whether the presence of various traits was, in fact, related to success in the managerial job, as writers since Henry (1948) have maintained. He devised a test (described below) to measure traits, often associated in the literature with successful management. Table 4.1 shows the correlates he obtained from a sample of 306 American managers, with the traits frequently mentioned in the literature as having importance for managerial success.

Structure of research tool

Having looked at the purpose of the questionnaire, we turn to a brief description of the inventory itself. This consists of sixty-four pairs of words, thirty-two of equal positive, and thirty-two of equal negative value to the subject. The method of choosing the pairs of words is described by Ghiselli as follows:

> The test used in the present research was one developed a few years ago by the author and has been successfully used in a number of studies not only of managers but also of personnel in a wide variety of other types of occupations. The test consists of sixty-four pairs of personally descriptive adjectives. The adjectives

were chosen so that both members of each pair are similar in terms of the social desirability of the human qualities they symbolize. As a consequence, in taking the test the respondent tends to be prevented from just giving a favourable description of himself, and so must project something of his actual qualities in choosing between the two alternatives. In half of the pairs the individual checks that adjective which he believes most characterizes him, both adjectives referring to socially desirable traits. In the other half of the pairs he checks the adjective he believes least characterizes him, both adjectives in these pairs referring to socially undesirable traits. [p.33.]

The subject is asked to tick the word which most (or least) applies to him. For instance, he may consider himself to be both frank and affectionate but marginally more frank than affectionate, in which case he will tick the first. Similarly, he may not consider himself either shy or lazy, but even less shy than lazy, in which case he ticks shy. Analysis by the researcher of the words ticked by subjects well-known to him indicates that they tick the words one might expect, and thus give a reasonably 'accurate' word picture of themselves. This is not adduced as evidence, but is an interesting reflection on the process.

Each pair of words has been tested by Ghiselli to see which words are ticked a significant number of times by each of the control groups, so some words add to the score on more than one dimension.

The procedure is quite simple. Ten separate overlays are made — each one marked with the scoring key for one variable. Then the score for each variable can be easily computed, and converted into norms using a table constructed for the purpose. The scores can then be fed back to the participants in detail, or as an anonymous group.

Analysis of summary statistics

After coding, the results were analysed, using the statistical package for the social sciences. Table 4.2 shows that the results for British

Table 4.2 *Comparison of means and standard deviations for sub-samples*

	Manufacturer		Local government		Chain store		Insurance broker		British sample (612)		American managers (306)	
	Mean	SD	Mean	SD	Mean	SD	Mean	SD	Mean	SD	Mean	SD
N. Achievement	40.3	6.8	42.0	8.2	43.6	7.5	40.3	9.0	40.8	8.4	41.81	8.65
N. Self-actualisation	10.1	2.8	11.4	4.6	10.6	2.5	10.2	3.1	10.4	2.9	10.50	2.50
N. Power	9.8	1.9	9.7	2.2	10.6	2.2	10.7	2.0	10.3	2.1	10.80	2.17
N. Reward	5.0	2.1	5.6	2.2	4.4	2.0	5.2	2.2	5.0	2.2	4.05	1.85
N. Security	11.0	3.8	11.3	4.2	9.7	4.0	11.3	4.3	11.0	4.3	10.26	3.61
Sup. ability	27.7	6.1	29.1	5.9	29.4	6.7	26.4	6.2	27.8	6.1	30.46	6.26
Intelligence	42.6	7.8	45.6	6.3	42.5	6.7	41.6	6.7	42.6	6.8	41.61	7.57
Initiative	29.8	7.1	30.2	7.5	33.7	6.8	30.9	7.4	31.1	7.5	32.86	6.40
S-assurance	26.6	5.7	27.6	4.8	29.7	4.7	27.7	4.8	27.7	4.9	28.30	5.85
Decisiveness	19.6	4.2	18.0	4.2	20.4	5.5	18.1	4.9	18.8	5.1	22.23	4.85

managers were not very different from American managers tested, and justified Sekaran's (1981) remarks about the cultural transferability of managerial concepts. It will be observed that most of the mean scores are quite close and fall within each other's standard deviations. It should be noted that the lengths of the scales are different and therefore no comparison between items is possible at this stage. These scores have only been produced to show how comparable the raw scores are.

Not only are the raw scores for the whole sample close to Ghiselli's findings, but the sub-samples are also close, as Table 4.2 shows.

The means for the sub-samples and whole sample have been converted into percentile scores in Table 4.3. These scores reflect the range of scores achieved over the total sample and the distribution of scores over the range.

Table 4.3 *Table of percentile scores for sample and main sub-samples*

Trait	Manufacturer	Agency	Store	Broker	Average for total sample
N. Achievement	48	56	63	48	51
N. Self-actualization	53	68	59	54	56
N. Power	49	42	64	66	58
N. Reward	58	65	52	61	58
N. Security	54	57	52	57	54
Sup. Ability	52	60	62	44	52
Intelligence	52	69	52	47	52
Initiative	41	43	62	47	48
Self-assurance	45	52	68	53	53
Decisiveness	60	47	64	48	55

Before leaving this part of the data we must display one other piece of internal evidence to justify Ghiselli's theory that certain elements contribute towards managerial effectiveness. He states (p.165) that the more effective managers are those who score higher in the following attributes (in order of salience):

Supervisory ability
Need for achievement

Intelligence
Need for self-actualization
Self-assurance
Decisiveness
Lack of need for security
Initiative
Lack of need for high reward

Samples in one company of managers at three levels — top, senior and middle management — were obtained, and found to vary in approximately the direction indicated by Ghiselli. Table 4.4 shows the results.

Table 4.4 *Levels of management compared*

Trait	7 Directors		26 Senior Managers		94 Middle Managers	
	Mean	*SD*	*Mean*	*SD*	*Mean*	*SD*
N. Achievement	43.3	8.1	39.7	5.7	39.9	9.0
N. Self-actualization	11.7	2.7	9.8	3.0	9.9	3.3
N. Power	8.9	2.2	9.8	2.0	10.3	2.1
N. Reward	5.6	1.8	5.0	2.3	5.1	2.3
N. Security	8.7	3.0	12.0	3.6	11.6	4.4
Sup. Ability	27.6	4.7	27.6	7.1	27.5	6.6
Intelligence	45.6	7.7	42.7	7.0	42.3	6.7
Initiative	33.0	5.4	30.0	7.8	27.4	10.2
Self-assurance	28.7	5.7	25.2	6.0	27.3	4.9
Decisiveness	19.9	3.8	19.3	4.4	18.2	5.4

Comparing Ghiselli's prediction with these results we see that:

Sueprvisory ability is almost exactly the same at all levels.
Need for achievement is higher at the top level than for the other two.
Intelligence fits Ghiselli's prediction exactly.
Need for self-actualization is similar to the need for achievement results.
Self-assurance is higher at the top than at senior and middle levels.
Decisiveness fits Ghiselli's prediction exactly.

Need for security is lower at the top than at middle level: senior managers have higher needs than middle managers.
Initiative fits Ghiselli's prediction exactly.
Need for reward does not fit Ghiselli's prediction: top managers have higher needs than senior or middle managers.
Need for power fits Ghiselli's prediction exactly.

In summary, four of the ten items agree with Ghiselli's predictions; four work at two levels only; one is indeterminate and one is contraindicative.

If it is broadly true that the men who became directors were promoted to that level because they were more effective than the rest of the senior managers, and if it is broadly true that men appointed senior managers were more effective managers than the middle managers, then the difference in the scores of each group on the Ghiselli inventory is a further indication that these scales measure what they purport to.

Frequency Distribution

An important shortcoming of the Ghiselli inventory is the shortness of some of the scales which can lead to insensitivity of measurement. Table 4.5 gives, for each trait measured, minimum, interquartile and maximum frequencies, to give a visual idea of the degree of bunching that occurs in the data.

Table 4.5 *Frequency distribution for total sample*

Trait	Lowest score	Score at 25th percentile	Score at 50th percentile	Score at 75th percentile	Highest score	D–B / E–A	K
N. Achievement	9	36	41	46	62	.19	1.07
N. Self-act.	0	8	10	12	44	.09	26.71
N. Power	5	9	10	12	16	.27	−0.09
N. Reward	1	3	5	7	10	.44	−1.08
N. Security	2	8	11	14	22	.30	−0.59
Sup. Ability	14	23	28	32	55	.22	.27
Intelligence	17	39	43	48	61	.20	.04
Initiative	0	26	31	36	47	.21	1.73
Self-assurance	13	24	28	31	40	.26	.06
Decisiveness	5	16	19	23	33	.25	−0.40

The interquartile range as a proportion of total range is shown in the second to last column on the right of the table, and shows that, in most cases, the middle 50 per cent of the readings occurred over about a quarter of the total range. The kurtosis readings are also shown in the last column : only the second trait (N.self-actualization) has a highly bunched set of readings.

If we turn to the similar statistics for each of the sub-samples, we can compare the kurtosis readings for each and see how consistent these effects are.

So much for the direct scores. The next step is to examine how these scores relate to one another, and the obvious basic tool is the correlation coefficient, which tells us how far one trait is related to another. We can also pick out groups of traits that are all related to one another and so find words to describe various aspects of the data (known as factors). Then we can go on to see how these groups vary from company to company (known as the process of discrimination). For those readers who, like the author, are mathematicians by rote rather than intuition, we have given some space to the elementary process of analyzing coefficients because it gives a 'feel' for the flavour of the data and renders the more sophisticated methods of the computer more credible. It is also more 'hands-on' and thus somewhat more fun.

Correlations between traits

Table 4.5 sets out all the correlations in the sample with a probable significance of $p =$ or $< .001$. (i.e. almost certainly significant). The following remarks may be of assistance in reading the data:

(1) Need for power has only one significant correlate — self-assurance — and this is low enough to warrant the exclusion of need for power as a general tool for analysis. Much has been written about power in organizations but it remains an elusive concept, unrelated to considerations of effectiveness as Litwin showed in his original study (reported in Litwin and Stringer (1968)).

(2) The only other missing correlation is that between intelligence

and decisiveness. We might, in this context, quote Hamlet:

> And thus the native hue of resolution
> Is sullied o'er with the pale cast of thought
> And enterprises of greath pith and moment
> With this regard their currents turn awry,
> And lost the name of action [III:i.]

(3) There is a 'nest' of high correlations between five items, as follows:

	N. self. act.	N. sec.	Initiative	Self-assurance
N. ach.	.469	−.548	.580	.549
N. self-act.		−.663	−.564	−.508
N. security			−.563	−.442
Initiative				.546

This indicates that strongly achievement-orientated managers (whether the achievement is the development of the self or the improvement of his status) are those with low need of security, strong initiative and strong self-asurance. When the total matrix is compared with Ghiselli's total matrix for 306 managers, it will be seen that in the majority of cases the correlations are quite similar. The main exception is the case of supervisory ability: with the American managers the links between this ability and achievement need, decisiveness and intelligence are much closer than in Britain. An American manager with a strong need to achieve is likely to be a more intelligent and capable supervisor than his British counterpart. Reassured that the British sample is internally consistent with the American sample, we turn to an analysis of the four sub-samples.

Manufacturing company correlations

The statistics for this company show one or two interesting characteristics. First, it is the only group where none of the drives is

Table 4.6 *Correlation coefficients for American and British managers*

Trait	N. self-act.	N. power	N. reward	N. security	Sup. ability	Intelligence	Initiative	Self-assurance	Decisiveness
N. Achievement	.43(.47)	.02(.08)	−.41(−.37)	−.54(−.55)	.52(.36)	.59(.47)	.59(.58)	.47(.55)	.52(.44)
N. Self-act.		.04(−.01)	−.21(−.28)	−.62(−.66)	.37(.35)	.42(.42)	.44(.56)	.35(.51)	.37(.36)
N. Power			.16(−.01)	−.08(−.13)	−.04(−.02)	.03(.08)	.11(.12)	.19(.14)	.12(.04)
N. Reward				.18(.25)	−.18(−.32)	.03(.16)	−.51(−.58)	−.19(−.30)	−.29(−.40)
N. Security					−.52(−.50)	−.33(−.31)	−.35(−.56)	−.25(−.44)	−.39(−.44)
Sup. Ability						.36(.22)	.35(.38)	.29(.35)	.45(.33)
Intelligence							.30(.19)	.40(.41)	.24(.03)
Initiative								.43(.55)	.41(.44)
Self-assurance									.42(.36)

Key: UK in brackets

associated with supervisory ability. This would seem to indicate that this faculty is not one which is sought after by the company in a consistent manner. On the other hand, it is the only group to relate all drives to intelligence, as if this was the overriding requirement in company personnel; the same applies to decisiveness.

The model for the culture then becomes one of seeking to attract self-assured, decisive people and, by means of stimulating their need for achievement and need for self-actualization, improve their intelligence. Table 4.7 gives some support to this theory (need for security correlates negatively with all elements).

Table 4.7 *Intercorrelations for the manufacturing company*

Trait	N. self-act.	N. security	Intelligence	self-assurance	Decisiveness
N. achievement	.43	−.49	.48	.63	.51
N. self-act.		−.48	.42	.51	.51
N. security			−.42	−.42	−.39
Intelligence				.42	.09*
Self-assurance					.46

* not significant at .001 level (all others are)

Correlations for the local government agency

The correlations for this group again hold interesting facts. First, it is the only organization where achievement is not related to reward. Secondly, there is no relationship between the need for self-actualization and the need for achievement — probably because of the two sub-cultures within the organization, one professional and self-actualizing, and the other administrative and achievement-orientated — and this division is more pronounced here than elsewhere. Those with professional orientations emerge as more likely to have supervisory ability than those without (coefficient of correlation = .37) and this again is a suprising result, until one recalls that administrators do not have to do so much supervision as technical staff. Self-actualizers also are not necessarily self-assured and this makes them different from the other companies' administrators.

It is interesting that, in the agency, the need for security correlates highly and negatively with initiative. Those members of the organization with high security needs will certainly be lacking in initiative, and one would be tempted to suppose that the need for security is a primary motivation, were it not for other data.

Decisiveness is a special concept for this culture. It correlates positively with both supervisory ability and initiative and this relationship, although not supported by a strong correlation between supervisory ability and initiative yet shows that the three elements move together. Stronger supervisory ability is more necessary in the agency than elsewhere, since the culture, while discouraging initiative, does not support leadership. The cultural model in the agency is thus described by these statistics as seeking people of decisive ability, who will not be destroyed by the indecisive culture, and who may be given jobs where they can supervise and take initiatives. The converse is more likely, however — that it will attract people whose need for security is paramount and this will depress the urge to achieve and to lead. The correlation table is shown in Table 4.8.

Table 4.8 *Intercorrelation for the Agency*

Trait	N. Security	Initiative	Decisiveness
N. achievement	−.58	.66	.47
N. security		−.64	−.38
Initiative			.45

Correlations for the retailing group

This set of statistics is exceptional in four ways: supervisory ability is highly correlated with achievement need (i.e. 'if you wish to get on you must be able to command others' —unsurprising, given the large number of people employed in stores); no correlations between achievement and decisiveness ('decisions are made at the centre only'); the need for security is not highly correlated with intelligence; and supervisory ability is closely linked with self-assurance — a reflection upon the kind of supervisor required, and a direct contrast to that obtaining in the agency.

When we come to look for a cultural pattern in the stores we find it is far weaker; only N.achievement, N.security, self-assurance and supervisory ability are evident.

Table 4.9 *Stores' correlation coefficients*

Traits	N. security	Sup. ability	Self-assurance
N. Achievement	−.57	.40	.42
N. Security		−.47	−.44
Sup. Ability			.41

The inference here is that the culture demands people with self-assurance to which it will impart supervisory ability, a simple culture in which intelligence is valued as a correlate of self-assurance and stimulated by needs for achievement and self-actualization.

Correlations for the insurance broking company

These are unusual in their conformity. Alone among the main sub-samples this has a nest of coefficients exactly similar to the total sample, as the following Table 4.10 shows. In other words, alone among the sub-samples, the broker has no cultural bias. This will show up more clearly in the discriminant analysis.

Table 4.10 *Correlation coefficients between five variables for the main sub-samples*

Traits		N. Self-act.	N. Sec.	Initiative	Self-assurance
N. Achievement	Total	.47	−.55	.58	.55
	Company	.50	−.59	.54	.51
N. Self-act.	Total		−.66	.56	.51
	Company		−.75	.63	.50
N. Sec.	Total			−.56	−.44
	Company			−.58	−.43
Initiative	Total				.55
	Company				.58

Conclusion

The correlations have at least given us four crude types of character trait grouping that we may now call

(1) Simple, supervisory (stores)
(2) Intelligent, self-actualizing (agency)
(3) Intelligent, decisive (manufacturing)
(4) Nondescript (insurance broking company)

In the next section we shall see how the use of discriminant analysis throws up differences in the composition of the sub-samples.

Meaning of the data

So far we have examined the tissue of the data and seen how each set of data manifested its own characteristics even at an elementary level. Now we can probe somewhat deeper. Our first question must be: does the body of data have any real meaning beyond that of the self-descriptive inventory? Can it be related to what is known, or hypthesized, about people? To get at the roots of the data we used the technique known as factor analysis. In this technique groups of variables which move together are separated into sets, each set embracing a decreasing part of the data, until the sets become too small to be reliable for intepretation. The sets of variables are the 'nests' that were observed in chapter three only created with more mathematical precision. The variables themselves are expressed as relationships to the central factor in much the way way as the struts of a half-opened umbrella are related to its stick: only in this umbrella most of the struts are at unequal distances from the stick. Since not all the struts will conveniently cluster round one stick there arises the possibility of making two or three and sometimes four 'umbrellas' using those struts left over, and here a confusion may arise because it may be difficult for the computer to decide whether a strut which does not obviously belong to the first set belongs to the first or second set. In order to prevent this overlap, the computer introduces a new rule, called 'Varimax', stipulating that all 'sticks' must be arranged at right angles to one another. In this way the possibility of overlap is minimized and the first 'umbrella' tends to lose struts to the others. In his analysis, Ghiselli did not avail himself of this technique; consequently, he viewed the first factor as the answer to the problem of what constituted an effective manager, as if there were only one set of attributes characterizing him.

Using orthogonal rotation — the Varimax solution — we see that there is more than one. All the managers in the sample were seen by their organizations as effective enough to warrant promotion to senior levels — they were clearly not identical — hence it is reasonable to assume that each factor represents a different kind of effectiveness. The first factor represents the most common type, but the others are also valid descriptions of managerial effectiveness.

Principal factor analysis

Table 4.11 shows the principal factor analysis for the sample. There are only two significant factors (Eigenvalue equal to or greater than 1.0) and it will be seen that the first factor contains more variables with high value than the second. As will be seen from column three of the table, the factor coefficients of factor 1 match the profile of correlations' coefficients found by Ghiselli to exist between raw scores and job success of managers.

It should, perhaps, be observed that, according to experts, these are quite good correlations for the type of work. As Guion (1965) pointed out: 'One learns not to expect very large correlations in personnel work; average validity coefficients for different types of tests and for different kinds of jobs and with different kinds of criteria are in the .30s and low .40s' (p. 138).

Table 4.11 *Principal factor matrix with iterations*

Traits	Factor 1	Factor 2	Ghiselli's correlation between scores and job success
N. achievement	.742	.089	.34
N. self-actualisation	.721	.119	.26
N. Power	.106	.042	.03
N. reward	−.510	.595	−.18
N. security	−.833	−.075	−.30
Supervisory ability	.532	−.049	.46
Intelligence	.447	.760	.27
Initiative	.784	−.222	.15
Self-assurance	.674	.111	.19
Decisiveness	.542	−.239	.22

Table 4.12 *Varimax rotated factor matrix*

Traits	Factor 1	Factor 2	Factor 3
N. achievement	.458	531	.312
N. self-actualisation	.314	.427	.511
N. power	.036	.088	.064
N. reward	−.806	.068	−.103
N. security	−.221	−.252	−.942
Supervisory ability	.320	.209	.381
Intelligence	−.159	.886	.129
Initiative	.678	.308	.356
Self-assurance	.410	.520	.259
Decisiveness	.476	.098	.339

Varimax solution

However, when the Varimax solution is obtained, a quite different picture emerges, as shown in Table 4.12. This table is different from the previous one in that all three factors now have large values in them, not just the first. We may therefore suppose that there are three elements in managerial success, underlying the principal factor and masked by it. The first factor has its highest elements initiative and low need for reward. This seeems to correspond to success at junior management level and these are backed up by relatively high self-assurance, decisiveness and motivated by significant need for achievement. For the sake of convenience we label this type of manager the 'fixer'.

In the second factor we see a somewhat different pattern. Here intelligence has a very heavy weighting, backed up by considerable self-assurance and motivated by relatively powerful needs for achievement and self-actualization. Need for security is somewhat less than for the 'fixer', as is initiative. We have given the soubriquet 'consultant' to this factor since there is a positive need for reward and very low weighting for decisiveness.

The final factor is the strongest in supervisory ability with relatively weak intelligence, but backed up by moderate weighting for initiative, self-assurance and decisiveness. The need for self-actualization is strongly loaded and need for security is highly negative. It is relatively easy to make sense of these loadings. It is known that good supervisors are not necessarily 'witty in themselves' (e.g. Belbin (1981)) and self-actualization is more likely to be the motivation for a successful leader than need for achievement because good leadership speaks to the person rather than the task. Similarly, a good leader must be seen to be 'free-standing' and not hindered in his behaviour by the need for self-preservation. We have, therefore, called this factor 'supervisor'.

Individual companies

We might expect these three factors to appear in all samples of successful management and this proves to be the case for all major sub-samples, but occurring in different order, as shown in Table 4.13.

Table 4.13 *The order in which the three main factors occur in the sample*

		Fixers	Consultants	Supervisors	Deviant form
Total sample	(612)	1	2	3	
Senior managers' course at Centre	(54)	1	3	2	4*
Insurance broker	(101)	2	3	1	
Local government agency	(74)	2	3	1	
Chain stores	(74)	2	3	1	
Manufacturing	(43)		1	3	2†

Notes: * This disparate sub-sample taken from four senior managers' courses at the Centre yields a fourth factor — strong need for power and decisiveness. The manipulative manager?

† For manufacturing seniors the highest loadings are on need for reward, intelligence and lack of initiative — perhaps the stereotype company man!

The first point to note is that the order of three of the four main sub-samples is the same: supervisors, followed by fixers, followed by consultants. This is probably because the nature of such jobs is supervisory — they are senior managers. Secondly, the order for the sample as a whole ranks fixers highest. This may be because in the rest of the sample the seniority is somewhat less than in the sub-samples. The reason for the difference in the order for the manufacturing company may lie in the fact that this sub-sample included some very senior managers indeed (the top board). Or it may be because it is a manufacturing not a service organization like the others.

Factor analysis free of organizational norms

Evidence for the interaction between organizational norms and character traits is provided by the data from public senior management courses at the Centre. A total of fifty-four managers from a wide variety of organizations completed the inventory. Thus the organizational norms (or cultural element) could not have had any effect upon the data. Table 4.14 shows the very high loadings on the specific elements of initiative, supervisory ability and intelligence for the four-factor analysis of these managers (Eigenvalue minimum: 1.00).

Table 4.14 *Four-factor analysis of SMDP 78–81 (Varimax)*

	Factor 1	Factor 2	Factor 3	Factor 4
N. achievement	.53	51	.30	−.01
N. self-actualization	.75	.01	.35	−0.4
N. power	.01	.00	−.02	.59
N. reward	−.36	−.69	.06	.23
N. security	−.60	−.27	−.24	−.28
Supervisory ability	.03	.70	.19	.18
Intelligence	.18	.10	.79	.00
Initiative	.90	.28	−.04	−.16
Self-assurance	.45	.26	.39	.02
Decisiveness	.52	.08	.13	.33
Variance accounted for:	41.1%	12.7%	11.2%	10.1%

The analysis throws up a power-seeking manager: but although it is a significant type, accounting for 10.1 per cent of the variance, we do not encounter it again in our exploration. The fixer accounts for by far the largest variance, probably because these managers came mainly from the hearts of large organizations, and were not so senior as might be expected.

Comparison with other studies

It may be concluded that:

(1) There are three identifiable types of manager — the fixer, the supervisor and the consultant.

(2) At business schools dealing with managers from a variety of cultures, a fourth factor — manipulation — comes into play.

(3) At courses for middle management, where membership of the course is secured by successful performance, the supervision factor is most clearly in evidence, followed by the fixer factor.

(4) Only among the most senior line management did the consultant emerge as the leading factor.

These indications of discrete styles are borne out by the work of Stamp (1981), who found that there existed several levels of problem-solving ability among managers and these corresponded both to the position of the manager in his company and his intellectual ability. The levels isolated here may correspond with her levels, two, three and four, typified as follows:

Type B   *Pragmatic Analysis*: the person solves problems by adopting a trial and error approach.

Type C   *Analytic Intuition*: 'the person oscillates between "being with" the experience and standing back from it in order that extra knowledge and analysis be brought to bear' (ibid., p.290). The words used by Stamp mirror the 'helicopter quality' developed for Shell by Muller (1970) on which a whole philosophy of supervisor training has been built (see particularly pp.29–33).

Type D   *Conceptual Analysis*: People use conceptual frameworks to solve the problem, they emphasize logical analysis and detachment. 'A person with this type of capability tends to be seen as a specialist and will often excel in research on staff or consultancy areas' (Stamp, ibid., p.291).

Given that these three types exist embedded in the mass of management, it is reasonable to suppose, with Newman (1953) and others, that if you change the people or balance of people, you change the culture. He gave examples of how the chief executives of organizations have changed the mix of personnel to emphasize a particular philosophy or social objective, and concluded (p.242) that 'there is real meaning in the expression "He is our kind of man" '.

A similar attempt was made by McFeely (1971) to distinguish a 'three-ply' management system. At the IDEATIONAL level, the main activities would be the creation and development of philosophy, ideology and perception or image: the idioms used would be corporate objectives, profit centres and the establishment of key task areas; and the most common patterns of interaction would be within the management team, and also the outside world. At the SYNERGISTIC level, the main activities would be transitional, catalytic and enabling; the idioms would be systems, programmes and goals and the patterns of interaction would be based upon professionalism. At the PROCESS level, the main activities would be to do with operations and technology; the idioms would be housekeeping and observance of schedules, and the patterns of interaction would be homeostatic. These levels correspond closely with the three types isolated in this reasearch.

Kirton (1980) has for several years been investigating two contrasting types of creativity, problem-solving and decision-making. Using his thirty-two item inventory, in which there is a five-point response range to each item, he has shown that there are two main types of manager whom he calls 'adaptors' and 'innovators'. Adaptors are those managers who 'tend to operate cognitively within the confines of the appropriate consensually accepted paradigm within which a problem is generally perceived. Innovators, by contrast, are more liable to treat (formally or intuitively) the enveloping paradigm as part of the problem' (p.213–14). He stated that whereas adaptors change by adjustment, innovators change by challenge and thus 'have more trouble in gaining acceptance for their definition of the problem and also for the solutions that they offer' (p.214).

The parallels between these types of our fixers and consultants are extremely close. Kirton reported two studies: one is not very convincing statistically, the other highly so. The study carried out at a Canadian business school on managers who had elected to go on the course showed that 'line' managers tended to be *adaptive* and 'staff' managers *innovative*. He concluded, first, that adaptors and innovators are both needed by organizations, and second, that although organizations whose selection process favours 'high fliers' will tend to pick 'innovators', the socialization process that takes place in the first years may cause them to leave. This coincides with our own findings in the research. He also hypothesized, but had no data to prove it, that the mix will vary according to environmental turbulence. (Emery and Trist, 1965).

In a subsequent study, using Kirton's methodology, Hayward and Everett (1983) showed that 'adaptive' local government officers were more likely to be promoted than 'innovators', unless the latter were selected for some specific purpose. They found that junior staff were more innovative than senior staff and that younger staff (aged twenty-one to twenty-four) were more innovative than older staff (thirty and above). They concluded that people 'leave an organisation, or stay, according to whether the organisation suits their personality' (p.341).

A most exhaustive study of managers that also covers a large number of managers is Stewart's 1967 study of managers and their jobs. The sample was 160 managers of various levels of seniority and the diary was self-administered. By using cluster analysis three groups of managers were identified. The first two were remarkable either for the time spent away from the firm or for the time spent 'in solitary paperwork'. Managers in the third group 'whose main job was to supervise and coordinate the work of other people in the company' (p.134) were sub-divided into three groups: 'discussers' (who were 'nearest to the sample average' and 'spent a relatively high proportion of their time with colleagues'); 'man managers' (also known as 'trouble-shooters') who spent 'nearly all their internal contact time with their subordinates'; and 'committee-men' who, according to Stewart, all 'worked for large companies' (p.122) and had 'a wide range of internal contacts with people in other departments and in a variety of different levels in the organisation' (p.134). The examples Stewart gave were of people with specialized jobs, and the 'typical' case history she presented was a manager whose major preoccupation at the time of the study was 'longer-term planning for expansion, coupled with reorientation of the organisation towards larger scale production of a smaller variety of equipment' (p. 126). It is perhaps significant that the three sub-types of the managers in group three correspond quite adequately to the fixers, supervisors and consultants of this study. Her managers were evenly divided between sub-groups three and four (35 & 33) respectively, but there were, as in this study, far fewer memebrs in group five (14 only). Half of these tended to work in the more technologically advanced firms, chemicals and electronics. It seems, therefore, that either people choose patterns of work that correspond to their own personality traits and needs, or that the balance of types of people employed varies from industry to industry. Certainly in her classification there was no discrimination according to job. (There are production control managers in categories three and five; there are works managers in three and four; and there are works engineers in categories four and five.) Nor does there need to be, if the psychological explanation is accepted. Similar explanations might be fitted to other studies, were sufficient data available.

Discriminant analysis

This analysis, however, while telling us something about the nature of effective managers, and grounding the data in what is known about levels of effectiveness, does not effectively distinguish one organization from another. Another basically simple technique can be used to pursue this line of investigation. It consists in deriving from the data for each manager a number of functions which distinguish the organizations from each other. In the first instance data from only three organizations was used and it was possible to distinguish them using two functions only. The organizations were: the retail store chain; the local government agency; and the manufacturing firm. The two functions are shown in Table 4.15. Using these two functions it is possible to calculate the group mean for each of the three groups, which are reasonably different as Table 4.16 shows, with only the manufacturing company failing to achieve

Table 4.15 *Standardised canonical discriminant function coefficients for three organizations*

Trait	Function 1	Function 2
N. achievement	.13306	.73589
N. self-actualization	.78387	.45089
N. power	−.24139	.19541
N. reward	.39481	.34304
N. security	.68184	.57433
Supervisory ability	.24646	.36933
Intelligence	.33843	−.56494
Self-assurance	−.55091	.65824
Decisiveness	−.28795	−.43763

Table 4.16 *Functional coefficients for three organizations*

Organization	Function 1	Function 2
Manufacturing	−.04781	−.47888
Stores	−.55450	−.15348
Agency	+.61288	+.12479

a significantly large score on Function 1, but achieving a large score on the second. The functions may be conceptualized by looking at the largest loadings. In the case of Function 1 these are: need for self-actualization, need for security and low self-assurance — a rough profile of an 'administrator' in a large bureaucracy. The second function loads heavily on need for achievement, need for security, lack of intelligence and self-assurance — a rough profile of a proactive, perhaps unintellectual manager. Applying the coefficients to the functions, we might say that a typical stores' manager (−.5545 on the first function) would be the very reverse of administrative, whereas the agency manager would be administrative. The manufacturing manager would appear to be somewhat intellectual in approach (negative function score and negative group centroid score) and also fairly decisive, but devoid of motivation as it is understood in this questionnaire.

This division appears to allow the computer to predict the membership correctly of over half the three sub-samples, as Table 4.17 shows.

Table 4.17 *Discrimination classification results*

Actual group	No. of cases	Predicted group membership Manufacturing	Stores	Agency
Manufacturing	43	18 41.9%	12 27.9%	13 30.2%
Stores	74	16 21.6%	44 59.5%	14 18.9%
Agency	74	17 23.0%	14 18.9%	43 58.1%

Percentage correctly classified: 54.98

Having established some clear differences between people in three apparently strong and diverse cultures, a discriminant analysis was performed with the insurance broker added to the other three.

Table 4.18 *Discriminant function coefficients for four companies*

Traits	Function 1	Function 2	Function 3
N. self-actualization	.58712	.67989	.40733
N. power	−.41268	.42891	.14855
N. reward	.17495	.30184	.34938
N. security	.61806	.32745	.39681
Supervisory ability	.33132	−.42297	.49093
Intelligence	.62689	−.44259	−.22020
Self-assurance	−.62174	−.06315	.83541
Decisiveness	−.06072	−.49256	−.42150

Table 4.18 shows what happened. First, in order to accommodate the new company a third factor is needed. This means that conceptualization needs to be carried out in three-dimension space: the four quadrants become eight zones. Second, the addition of another service organization relegates the manufacturer to the third function (see Table 4.19).

Table 4.19 *Coefficients of group centroids*

Organization	Function 1	Function 2	Function 3
Manufacturing	.37531	.20421	−.48887
Stores	−.48102	−.36809	.07628
Agency	.64916	−.03354	.17135
Broker	−.24581	.36099	−.02170

According to this table the manufacturer and the agency resemble one another on the first function, as do the stores and the broker. The manufacturer and the stores resemble one another on the second function and are different from the broker. And the third function, as we have said, describes the manufacturer alone. So if the manufacturer is eliminated from the analysis we can discriminate between public sector agency and the private sector firms on the first function and between the two private sector firms on the second.

So how do we conceptualize the functions? The first loads heavily on (has as its highest value) the variables need for self-actualization, *negative* need for power, need for security, intelligence and lack of self-assurance. People with these attributes would be likely to be found in bureaucratic organizations such as the agency (and, incidentially, the manufacturer). You would not expect to find them in a selling business because they would find the pressures intolerable. We call this function 'bureaucratic tendency'.

Consider now the second function, which discriminates between the private sector organizations. All the drives load negatively, all the characteristics positively. The broker's men are ego-driven, according to the centroid values, and the storemen are distinguished for their ability to supervise, their intelligence and their decisiveness. So we may replace Harrison's original concept by four new ones: bureaucratic, anti-bureaucratic, ego-driven and managerial, adding if we wish the function for manufacturing which, since it loads positively on only two variables — intelligence and decisiveness — we can call problem-solving. This gives us the resolution shown in Table 4.20.

We have placed brackets around two words because the readings for the centroids are not above .3, and thus perhaps not so reliable.

Table 4.20　*Conceptualization of Tables 4.18 and 4.19*

Manufacturer:	Bureaucratic (managerial) problem-solving
Stores:	Anti-bureaucratic managerial
Agency:	Bureaucratic
Broker:	(Anti-bureaucratic) ego-driven

We can even picture each company as occupying one quadrant of a graph such as that shown in Figure 4.1. The manufacturer will ocupy the cube behind its quadrant, to signify the additonal problem-solving dimension.

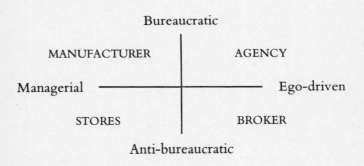

Figure 4.1　*Rationalization of Table 4.1*

What distinguishes these companies in real life? What causes them to employ people and train them to have characteristics which are commonly held but also different from other companies so that a 'sorting machine' can easily predict the nature of the corporate identity? One can make a few cautious assertions. The companies on the left of Figure 4.1 are more successful than those on the right in commercial terms. The companies at the top of the figure are larger than those at the bottom — so size plays its part in determination of culture. The strength of the stores' personnel is their ability to make a loose system work. The strength of the agency personnel is to work within a stifling atmosphere of constraint and yet preserve their souls. The brokers' strength is to be individuals. The strength of the manaufacturer is the ability to solve technical problems.

It would be all too easy to rest upon this simplistic rationalization. However, the model must be tested by the addition of other companies. To date we have information about three other organizations, two in the service sector (another insurance broker and the software division of a computer manufacturer) and one in both manufacturing and service (a transportation organization). Fortunately for this analysis, the centroids of these organizations behave as they should — the second broker situates midway between the first broker and the stores, the transportation organization is in the same quadrant as the manufacturer (although less well defined), and the software house, which claims to have a culture directly opposed to its rival the first manufacturer, is in exactly the opposite quadrant — ego-driven, anti-bureaucratic and not problem-solving.

It seems likely that the three dimensions isolated by the discriminant analysis — bureaucratic, managerial and problem-solving — are useful tools of culture classification.

Having established the current position of the organization, the next question will be to decide where it ought to be, and then offer some advice on getting there. These questions will be addressed in chapters seven and eight; the aim of this one has been to show how closely culture is linked with what the people of the organization are and what they have become because of doing their jobs sufficiently 'well' as to merit promotion to senior positions.

5 Improving the diagnosis

Introduction

We have so far shown that:

(1) Ghiselli's general conclusions about effective managers are supported, but conceal three or four separate factors.
(2) These factors correspond to three different sets of personality characteristics which may affect problem-solving behaviour.
(3) The combinations of the managers of the three factor types vary from firm to firm. There is some evidence that they vary according to level.
(4) It is possible to distinguish managers in one organization from those in another with reasonable certainty, using either their character traits or their needs. Neither is more reliable than the other.
(5) The notion of an organizational culture is therefore linked to the perceptions of the managers belonging to an organization, and may not exist in objectively measurable form.
(6) Organizations in the service sector attract broadly similar kinds of people, irrespective of the market sector; and the characteristics of these people are different from those in the manufacturing sector.

In the process, a simple taxonomy of organizational cultures as derived from their employees has been developed, as follows:

Bureaucratic   (high or low)
Managerial   (high or low)
Problem-solving   (high or low)

This gives a total of eight possible cultures, and the research has thrown up four clear examples in manufacturing, local government, chain stores and insurance broking. However this evidence is all internal and we require evidence of a more general nature that these cultures exist discretely.

Some models of culture

Perhaps the best-known culture model is that of Harrison (1972) who recognized four cultures (power, role, task and atomistic). He did not seek to interrelate the cultures in any way except, perhaps, along a dimension such as the Tannenbaum–Schmidt power-sharing continuum, and even this does not sit very happily. Whereas it would be possible to argue that, for instance, bureaucratic-ego-driven is the same as the role culture, we should be arguing from prior knowledge since our bureaucratic example is a bureaucracy.

A further avenue of approach might be to classify organizations according to the way they learn. Kolb (1976), following Jungian psychology, devised a simple taxonomy of learning styles based upon the way organizations learn and these four combinations (sensation versus intuition and thought versus feeling) can be loosely calibrated with the four cultures identified by Harrison. Subsequent work by Carlsson *et al.* (1976) and Wolfe and Kolb (1979) gives support to this

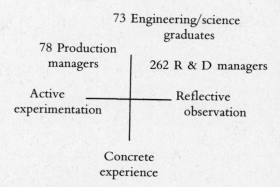

Figure 5.1 *Preferred learning styles by managerial type*
Source: Joney and Mumford (1982)

as a view of organization culture dictated by technology. However, this model, although it springs from the personality types observed by Jung, does not ascribe causality.

An adaptation of the Kolb Learning Styles Questionnaire has been used by Honey and Mumford (1982) on 1,302 British managers and they have devised norms which support this model. Figure 5.1 shows the first and second preferred learning styles of selected managerial types. We have eliminated samples where the second style was the one at the opposite end of the continuum (e.g. ninety-three marketing managers were said to have both active experimentation *and* reflective observations styles: this seems to indicate that two types of marketing manager were included in the sub-sample).

The general findings were as follows:

Kolb classification	Mean score
1 Concrete experience	9.3
2 Reflective observation	13.6
3 Abstract conceptualization	12.5
4 Active experimentation	13.7

It will be seen that 2 and 4 cancel out (just as Jung found equal propensity to introversion and extroversion) but abstract conceptualization was the next highest. There was a poor correlation between the Honey and Mumford LSQ and the Kolb LSI on concrete experience, and this may account for the low mean score for this category. Furthermore, by far the largest sub-sample was that of the R & D managers (20.1 per cent) so perhaps the findings were skewed. Certainly, those sub-samples that could be sited fit well with the description given in Myers Briggs ISTJ for Production Managers and INTJ for Innovators.

Hofstede's (1980) model contained a psychological model somewhat similar to the one expounded in this book but based upon cross-cultural rather than intra-cultural differences. It may be a useful framework but does not have immediate application, and Hunt (1981) was critical of this; he seemed to prefer a model involving centralization (or lack of it) and formalization (or lack of it).

The Harrison view of organizational culture has one possibly serious defect: it may not be describing culture at all, but simply four interpretations of organizational life. This would explain why students, asked which organizational culture they would prefer, tend to choose his 'task' culture. In a lengthy attempt to argue for a dynamically antitethical view of organization theory, Astley and Van de Ven (1983) postulated four views of organization and management, as follows:

(i) The natural selection view
According to this view, organizations are created and determined by environmental competition. Behaviour within them is random, natural or economic and the managerial role is inactive.

(ii) The strategic choice view
According to this view, people and their relationships are organized and socialized to serve the choices and purposes of those in power. Behaviour within them is constructed, autonomous and enacted and the manager's role is proactive.

(iii) The system-structural view
According to this view, roles and positions are hierarchically arranged so as to achieve the objective of the system efficiently. Behaviour is determined, constrained and adaptive and the manager's role is reactive.

(iv) Collective-action view
According to this view, organizations consist of communities or networks of semi-autonomous partisan groups that interact to modify or construct their collective environment, rules and options. Behaviour is reasonable, collectively constructed and politically negotiated. The manager's role is interactive.

Accepting, for the moment, the possibility of these four independent views, we may ask whether the Harrison model is not simply the symbolization of these differing views of organization. What if they were not cultures at all, but different labels for these views, respectively atomistic (natural selection); power (strategic choice); role (system-structural) and task (collective action)? Then we should have to determine culture in terms of the view of the world (*Weltanschauung*) accepted within that organiztion, and this might make more sense than simply relying on the four cultures as the only possible ones, since they have been generated from four structural possibilities. This method also enables us to take parts of each view and combine them to form a number of composite cultures. Thus the retailing group may have a strategic choice view of the world internally (e.g. self-assurance, need for power) and also a natural selection external view, depending on the niche the organization perceives itself to occupy in the retail store sector. This would cause the managers to value achievement, and thus express themselves by achievement. Similarly, the local government agency, built upon a system-structural view of the world, may also reflect the need for conflict within the organization. In this light, the four apparently discrete views are simply bases for multiple views based upon a view of one's own organization and a view of other organizations.

So culture depends once again on a self-image and the view of the self as part of an organization. Should one of these two become insignificant the dynamic truism is lost, and the culture becomes an ineffective proposition. In this sense culture is born out of the need to reconcile apparent discontinuities between the inner workings of organization and the external realities of the market place. We can now proceed to redefine the concept of culture as the difference between the logical internalization of effective operation as defined by the market and the preferred operating mode as evinced by the people within the organization, due to the selective processes that caused them to be there.

A different view may be taken of the four Harrison models. They may be stages in the life cycle of an organization as suggested by Quinn and Cameron (1983). Quinn and Cameron take nine life-cycle studies and show that each can be rationalized to four main stages:

(1) Entrepreneurial
This includes the marshalling of resources with entrepreneurial activities. The prime mover has power ('one-man rule'), and there is little planning and co-ordination. This approximates to the 'power' culture.
(2) Collectivity
In this stage, there is still informal communication and structure,

still a sense of mission and high commitment. There are long hours of work with modest rewards. This still approximates to the power culture.

(3) Formalization and control

At this stage we have formalization of rules, a stable structure, emphasis upon efficiency and maintenance and conservation with institutionalized procedures. This approximates to the role culure.

(4) Elaboration of structure

In this stage we see elaboration of structure, decentralization, adaptation and renewal. This is similar to the task culture.

The words used are interesting in themselves, for they seem to support a possible theory that organizations begin by being highly market-dependent (power culture) then seek to become independent (role culture) and then once again seek new contact with the market as existing products or services come to the end of their life cycle.

A further interesting facet of this study is that it shows the power culture as not one but two cultures — entrepreneurial and

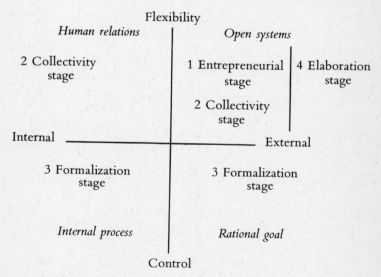

Figure 5.2 *Effectiveness values during the early stages of development*

collectivity. The authors theorize that the use of two dimensions — degree of control and attention to external stimuli — can allow different profiles of organizations to be drawn. They name their quadrants according to different models of organization, as shown by Figure 5.2.

This analysis, although not entirely convincing, does pose the question as to whether Harrison's cultures simply reflect the stages of development of an organization and, if so, whether he has provided a sufficient number of cultures. Certainly, his questionnaire tends to group the majority of organizations into the 'role' culture and this tends to reduce the utility of his instrument as a tool for measuring organization culture. If Quinn and Cameron are right in their summarization of other studies, we should provide for two 'power' cultures — entrepreneurial and collectivity. In this case the Harrison model would look somewhat like Table 5.1.

Table 5.1 *Combination of Harrison and Quinn-Cameron*

1 Formalisation	2 Elaboration	3 *Task*
4 Collectivity	5 (Uncultured)	6 Holdings
7 Entrepreneurial	8 (Emergent)	9 *Atomistic*

Harrison's names in italics.
New names in parentheses.

However, a more important aspect is the question raised by Quinn and Cameron regarding internal behaviour versus external behaviour. Can an organization be analysable as 'human systems' within the 'rational goal' outside? This theory leads to a possible explanation for the failure of the analysis to clearly define the manufacturer. Whereas it has a perfectly clear external image, yet the internal culture defies description by means of the Ghiselli protocol. One is forced to the conclusion that there are, in fact, two cultures — an inner culture used for dealing with internal problems and an outer culture used for dealing with the outside world.

A further possibility is that what we describe as culture is not a positive but a negative value: it simply explains the apparent discontinuity between what happens within the organization and what happens outside it. The literature of the subject suggests that there are three basic models of internal organization — high centralization, with high, medium and low formalization — which theoretically can produce three internal cultures, formalized, collective and entrepreneurial. There are also three possible theories about the environment: ordered society (where there is room for all sizes of firm and all levels of efficiency); Darwinian society (where the efficient firms destroy the inefficient ones) and inefficient society (where the Darwinian system fails to operate, for reasons of market inefficiency). If this is theoretically possible, then we have nine combinations of internal/external culture and we are free to site the companies in the sample at convenient distances from one another and to show diagrammatically the intuitive verity of their cultural differences.

Such an analysis of culture, while incomplete, gives some understanding of why cultures may differ even between closely related firms. One might suppose, for instance, that Marks and Spencer, British Home Stores and Woolworths would have the same, or nearly the same, culture. Intuitively they have not. The reason, according to this model, would be in each one's view of the market. Marks and Spencer sets out to dominate the markets in which it sells. BHS seeks a place in a market system for its own solution to the price-value optimization problem. Woolworths majors on low-price and assumes that the market prefers this attribute of goods to others.

If the foregoing is true, then we may write that culture is a function of the structure of the company and its view of the environment. But both these are created by the rulers of the company. We may therefore assume that their perception of the environment leads them to employ certain sorts of people and these people require certain kinds of structure. We thus have four elements of culture:

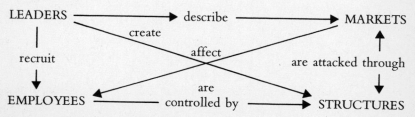

The relevance of this model is supported by the observation that organizations internalize their environments: they act as models of their constituent interest groups. For example, if the salesmen behave like their customers, the financial managers like their bankers, the buyers like their suppliers, and the brokers like their underwriters, it follows that the external climate will be re-enacted within the firm itself. Should the market be Darwinistic but the firm be structured very formally, then it follows from the model that the leaders will find themselves in an inappropriate posture and the employees likewise, and they will be apt to blame the leadership as inefficient or 'weak'. More interestingly, changes in market conditions will dictate changes in leadership style and changes in employee mix, so that the three types of managerial personality we have discerned will be perhaps more attuned to different types of market condition: the fixers will thrive in disordered markets; the consultants in ordered markets and the supervisors in inefficient markets where the goals of the organization are not clear. This is clearly a gross over-simplification, but the insight that emerges from these studies is that culture arises as much from the view of the world outside as from the shared attitudes and values about the firm itself. Something more objective is needed.

The key lies in a remark of Simon (1945) who contended that it is the psychological environment of decision-making that gives organizations their special meaning: 'Social institutions may be viewed as regularisations of the behaviour of individuals through subjection of their behaviour to stimulus-patterns socially imposed on them. It is in these patterns that an understanding of the meaning of function of organisation can be found' (p.109). This idea was taken up by Brousseau (1978) and then by Springer and Gable (1980) in a cross-cultural study to see how far motivation and structure were connected. 'Elaboration of existing theory and refinement of empirical data require specification of the combined effects of motivational and structural determinants of administrative behaviour' (p.671).

If, following Chandler (1962), we believe that strategy determines structure, and we also believe that strategy determines human resources, then the two are interlinked. In this case we must look for models containing elements of structure, as Hunt advised. In doing

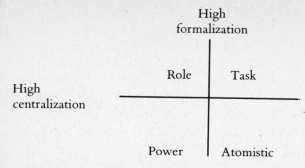

Figure 5.3 *Harrison's four cultures*

this, we may reappraise the existing models, theorizing about the relationships between Harrison's four cultures. We might arrange them around two axes entitled centralization and formalization, as shown in Figure 5.3. This would enable more accurate predictions to be made as to the likely culture of the service organization but leave us baffled about the manufacturing company. As Holdaway *et al.* (1975) have indicated (in connection with an Aston-type analysis of educational institutions), manufacturing firms seem to have different types of culture from service firms (see especially p.53ff). Similarly, although Simon and others have stressed the importance of environmental relationships, our studies so far have all revolved around the internal culture. While this is no bad thing in itself, since we do not wish to confuse the two cultures, yet we cannot forget the existence of the environment.

Weinshall (1977) has also found that a matrix much as the one we have described explains different types of structure. His names are entrepreneurial structure (informal and centralized), which leads to functional structure (formal and centralized), which leads to decentralized structure (formal and decentralized). He considers an organization that is informal and decentralized to be 'anarchical' (chaos or stagnation). The direction of development has been noted often in examining organizations (e.g. Graves (1981)).

Accordingly, it was decided to consult the largest body of organization data in the ESRC archive at Essex, to see whether information was available that would further elucidate the problem. Two studies were selected for this exercise — the original 1962–3 study carried out in the Birmingham area, and Child's 1967–9 study carried out over Great Britain. These two were selected because they used the original schedules and covered both manufacturing and services.

Together they provide a basic data bank of 134 organizations of which only eight are in the public sector. As will be shown in the ensuing paragraphs, the data do provide insights into the relation of centralization and formalization to type of organization. In the next section we will describe the results of an analysis according to structural characteristics.

Contextual Attributes of Service and Manufacturing Firms

In order to evaluate the contextual differences in firms having different structures, the organizations were divided into four sub-sets depending upon whether they were highly centralized or not, and highly formalized or not. This produced the breakdown shown in Table 5.2.

Table 5.2 *Centralization and formalization in the private sector*

Private sector	Service	Manufacturing
Low centralization: low formalization	12	10
High centralization: low formalization	8	30
High centralization: high formalization	8	14
Low centralization: high formalization	12	31
Total	40	85

Correlations were calculated for the 120 private sector firms along ten variables: as Table 5.3 shows, three of them correlated significantly with six of the nine others. The three variables are:

(i)   'Integration with suppliers', where the scale runs from 0, meaning irregular contacts, to 3, meaning ownerhsip of or by the supplier.

(ii)   'Sensitivity of output', where the scale runs from 0, meaning output to stock, to 4, meaning output controlled by client.

Table 5.3 *Highly intercorrelating variables*

Highly intercorrelating variables

Variable	1 Integration with suppliers	2 Sensitivity of output	3 Link with customers
Size	.191	n.s.	n.s.
Dependence on trade unions	.444	n.s.	−.210
Integration with suppliers	—	n.s.	−.165
Sensitivity of output	n.s.	—	.193
Specialisms contracted out	.292	−.191	n.s.
Link with customers	−.165	.193	—
Dependence *on* largest customer	n.s.	.179	.245
Dependence *of* largest customer	−.166	.149	.336
Specialization of function	.275	−.257	n.s.

All correlations significant at $p = < .05$.

(iii) 'Link with customers', where the scale runs from 0, meaning irregular links, to 3, meaning ownership of or by the customer.

This last variable correlates with the other two, although they do not themselves correlate ($−.0427$, $p = .318$).

Table 5.3 is interesting for two reasons: first, it shows that two important environmental input/output variables in columns 1 and 2 are closely connected with other forms of environmental dependence; and second that customer dependence has the opposite effect to supplier dependence: where these correlations are significant they are in the opposite direction. Furthermore, since customer link (column 3) is related positively to sensitivity of output (as one might expect) the inference is that even where the correlation for sensitivity is not significant (as in dependence on trade unions) the correlation is in the desired direction (the — non-significant — correlation for these two variables is .032). Thus, interdependence with suppliers produces one kind of effect — notably trade union problems and specialization — which are both strongly correlated ($p = 0$) with size; while dependence on customers produces a different effect — more generalization and less role specialization.

Where firms are dependent on neither suppliers nor customers (or dependent upon both) we may expect muddled relationships, and where the dependence changes we may expect culture changes. Take the case of the small housebuilder who is short of working capital. He will seek to obtain a contract for the sale of the house before he builds it (dependence on *customer*). His problem will be to obtain the materials once he has signed the contract. The large housebuilder, who can rely upon a certain number of sales per annum, must ensure that his supplies are secure. In doing so, he will sub-contract and sign long-term contracts (dependence on *supplier*). His main efforts are devoted to ensuring continuity of supply. As Table 5.3 shows, the size of the firm is not a significant element for customer dependence, but probably only the larger firms are interested in supply problems. The case is even more marked with single-source organizations such as oil companies, for small 'independents' can pick up crude oil on the spot market, whereas the large multinationals must ensure continuity of supply. This distinction is an important one for our understanding of organizations.

Service firms versus manufacturing firms

When the type of organization is introduced (service or manufacturing) quite a different picture emerges. For service organizations, the variable 'size' correlates significantly with five other variables, and 'dependence on the largest customer' with four, with the intercorrelation between the two relatively significant ($p = .022$ at $r = -.34.3$). Thus, so far as service organizations are concerned, we may isolate two types of firm, large dependent and small dependent such as a small advertising agency.

For manufacturing firms, only specialization of roles relates significantly to four of the other eight variables, so it may be concluded that there is little in the environment to cause culture effects. It is possible to conclude that for the culture of manufacturing firms the environment is not a significant element: dependence upon suppliers or customers does not entail polarization of other variables connected with the organization.

Armed with the theory that the culture in service organizations is connected with different elements from those in manufacturing organizations, we can now examine structural preferences according to variables, using analysis of variance, which tells whether the variance produced is significant for each of the variables. In the first instance the full sample for the 125 private sector firms was divided according to high or low centralization and high or low formalization. This produced the following spread:

	High formalization	
	22	43
High centralization		
	38	22

Then, for each variable, an analysis of variance was calculated. Five cases were found to be significant ($p < .05$).

Table 5.4 shows the mean scores for each structural type arranged in ascending order of size. This may be interpreted to mean that small firms are controlled by an individual; middle-sized firms are not

Table 5.4 *Mean scores for variables according to structure*

	High C Low F	Low C Low F	Low C High F	High C High F	Notes
Mean size (in thousands)	.9	1.2	2.1	5.2	
Degree of dependence on trade unions	1.3	1.4	1.5	2.7	Max. 4
Integration with suppliers	1.9	1.2	2.3	3.3	4 = ownership
Specialisms contracted out	6.2	7.8	10.0	8.8	Max. = 16
Specialization of roles	.4	.7	1.7	2.1	Max. 7

closely controlled and large firms are noticeable for the double-barrelled control mechanisms built into the structure. This corresponds to data collected using the Harrison questionnaire.

We can then see how far other variables are significantly linked to the main structural components. Dependence on trade unions follows the same pattern as size. As expected, the least structured firms are least integrated, but the High C–High F firms have very close links: 3.3 on a scale with a maximum of 4. So far as the variable 'specialisms contracted out' is concerned, it is noticeable that formalized organizations are more conscious of their boundaries than informal organizations; yet the largest organizations are not necessarily those that make the most use of sub-contractors. With the increased sub-contracting goes increased role specialization.

Taken as a whole, the data suggest that with increasing size comes:

(a) increasing complexity of organization,
(b) increasing role specialization, or the ability to distinguish what the firm can do from what it cannot,
(c) greater dependence upon outside suppliers,
(d) an ambivalent relationship with customers (no relationship significant).

Turning to the subsets, the picture is somewhat different.

Service organizations

The thirty-five service organizations of the private sector were distributed as follows:

High form

High cent

	3	12
	8	12

There is a bias away from structure and centralism. For this subsample three variables are significant (see Table 5.5.).

Table 5.5 *Mean scores for private sector service organizations*

	High C Low F	Low C Low F	Low C High F	High C High F	
Integration with supplier	1.5	.17	.75	4.3	
Sensitivy of output	2.0	2.0	2.0	1.3	Max. 4
Dependence on largest customer	.25	.50	.25	1.7	

As will be seen, integration with suppliers and dependence on largest customer is here linked with high centralization, a not unexpected finding. But the data is weak in explaining the culture of service sector organizations, as Holdaway *et al.* (1975) have pointed out.

Manufacturing organizations

There were ninety in the sample, distributed as follows:

High formalization

	19	31
High centralization		
	30	10

Most organizations used one structural dynamic extensively (thirty high cent., thirty-one high form.) but a greater proportion of companies were highly centralized (54 per cent versus 31.4 per cent) than in the service sector, maybe because of the technology.

As before, the main variables identified by ANOVA are indicated, in the same order (see Table 5.6). As will be seen, size, which was not seen as important in determining the structure of service organizations, is quite an important factor in manufacturing; the smallest and the largest are centralized and the middle sized companies are not. Formalization seems to be the prelude to greater growth (the mean size for low C/low F being almost the same as that for low C/high F,

Table 5.6 *Mean scores for manufacturing organizations*

	High C Low F	Low C Low F	Low C High F	High C High F
Size (thousands)	.7	2.0	2.1	5.5
Dependence on trade unions	1.5	2.5	1.9	2.8
Specialisms contracted out	6.3	7.9	10.7	8.7
Dependence of largest customer on organization	1.3	1.2	.9	1.8
Specialization	.3	1.5	2.1	2.1

but high C/high F shows a quantum leap to 5.5, more than double the mean size of the two intemediate stages).

The other figures are harder to interpret. Sub-contracting and specialization seem to be linked with formalization, as we have already seen. It becomes clear, however, that the overall picture shown in Table 5.6 is more or less an aggregation of two separate sets of variables: for manufacturing organizations the key variables are size, dependence on trade unions and specialization, and for service organizations, dependence upon suppliers and customers.

It is noteworthy that this conclusion can be reached by employing what amounts to split-half technique based upon the two main structural variables (centralization and formalization), which relates closely to size in the case of manufacturing but not in service organizations. The data do, however permit a mapping onto the four Harrison cultures:

1 High formalization and high centralization (the role culture) gives rise to different cultures, depending upon whether manufacturing or service is examined. In manufacturing the firm will probably be large, unionized, and independent of its market, while in the service sector, a role culture concentrates much more upon the identity of the supplier or client, and maintenance of the professional ethic.

2 The task culture (high formalization and low centralization) is not much different from the role culture in manufacturing, except that it is clearer in its sense of purpose (higher in specialisms contracted out) and less independent of the market. In

manufacturing one can imagine a task-type organization as being newly created (and therefore not highly unionized) organization making high-technology equipment for a wide variety of customers — impersonal, efficient and self-aware. Its counterpart in the service sector is equally marked by independence of its suppliers and customers. It has, perhaps, a specialized product — e.g. personal indemnity insurance, which it sells to a limited market. By contrast with its manufacturing counterpart, it can be quite small, and it is a culture often found in service organizations.

3 The power culture (high centralization and low formalization) in manufacturing is typically the small 'one-man band'. Non-specialized to a great degree, free of trade union interference, its essential aspect is its dominance of its largest customer. A local printworks for a newspaper would be an excellent example. In the service sector the firm is characterized by its integration with its supplier, such as a professional partnership, whose 'supplier' is the professional body, or an insurance broker with access to special underwriting facilities.

4 Atomistic (low centralization, low formalization). So far as manufacturing is concerned, this culture represents an intermediate stage between creation and permanence, perhaps engendered by the spirit of diversification. Its only remarkable feature would appear to be the high level of trade union activity. The culture may arise in the interim period between initial creation of the firm and its first radical reorganization; it represents the awkward stage of functional rationalization resultant from the takeover of one firm by another. In the service sector the atomistic type simply means a free-standing organization, such as a bookshop or property company. Its culture is that of independence and flexibility and an ability to change its business from one day to another, like the archetypal street-trader.

Conclusions from data collected by the 'Aston Group'

This analysis by main structural component has improved the

understanding of the original Harrison categories. It seems that they indicate different cultural patterns according to the nature of business (service or manufacturing). It is unfortunate that there is no reliable data in the ESRC Archive on a similar basis for public sector organizations but at least one is able to draw a distinction between service and manufacturing organizations: where technology is less important than people, the Ghiselli tool has good discriminating powers. We can further show that the service organizations discriminate in the order that one would expect from the Ghiselli, leaving room for separate studies on manufacturing.

Once again we are left with a need for at least a three-dimensional model to array the various cultures, even without benefit of any subjective or mythological data that might cause them to sub-divide further. And we are left in no doubt as to the importance of the environment as a determinant of culture.

We may now take the argument a stage further and say that culture is a function of the people working in the organization, the way the organization is arranged and the environment (economic and technological) in which it operates. If this is so, it is tempting to seek some goodness of fit between the three elements.

Here we are cautioned by the part of the research that bears upon types of organization person to be found by factor analysis. Much of the writing on career development (e.g. Schein (1978)) is concerned with the planning of viable careers, and the work of Stamp and others indicates that there is a set of different activities that may be hierarchically arranged. So the combination of types may be uncontrolled although control will certainly be attempted, as Silverman and Jones have so conclusively shown. These types are not new discoveries.

There are a number of studies that discover the same phenomenon, or something similar, ranging from the relatively narrative reports of Marshall and Stewart (1981) through Kotter (1982) — who identified fixers and supervisors — and Mintzberg (1982) who specified the role of the consultant type within organiztions, to Gill (1982) who investigated the intelligence factor among businessmen using statistical analysis. He concluded that there was 'an optimum (parabolic) range of intelligence for decision-making potential, a finding which is consistent with the more general level of "managerial success" with the findings of Ghiselli (1963) and Kraut (1969)' (p.145). All that is suggested here is that the mix varies according to where the organization is horizontally sliced.

So far as organization culture fit is concerned, Hofstede (1980), in advocating strong culture, is only following Dunnette and Campbell (1970) who claimed they were always able to relate the problems of ailing organizations to poor co-ordination, inefficient and inaccurate communication and poorly defined and transmitted organization objectives (p.351). Both may be guilty of over-simplification; they are referring to the outer, not the inner, culture.

The inner culture is important to understand because it is the one the person has to work in. A *Times Guide to Career Development* published 3 February 1983 warns: 'Companies may spend millions of pounds a year on the marketing of their products and yet neglect to tell job applicants anything really useful about the culture they may be joining. Yet learning the company culture and adapting to it may be a key factor in a successful career.' It doesn't, however, say how the company should go about this. Much research has gone into describing ways of measuring culture but, as has been shown, there is little convincing comparative work, apart from the descriptive work of such authors as Burns and Stalker (1961). By ascertaining that manufacturing cultures seem to occupy a different dimension from service cultures, and public from private (although this is less clear) we have at least enabled the reader to feel confident that the research is all pointing in the same direction although it is easier to analyze the factors than integrate the knowledge!

Throughout this chapter our own research has been kept in the background because it seemed easier to use the relatively simplistic approach adopted by Harrison. It may be remembered that our own research generated three dimensions (bureaucratic, managerial and problem-solving) yielding eight states as follows:

	1	2	3	4	5	6	7	8
Bureaucratic	High	High	High	High	Low	Low	Low	Low
Managerial	High	High	Low	Low	High	High	Low	Low
Problem-solving	High	Low	High	Low	High	Low	High	Low

How do these states reconcile with the cultures suggested by

Harrison? The mapping is apparently simple and it leads to a further insight. Harrison's role and task cultures seem to correspond to our bureaucratic and managerial dimensions respectively. But our research has shown that both dimensions are combined in several cases: e.g. the first state, which was the case for the manufacturing company, and the second state — the case of the rail transportation company. Similarly the power culture — which is the anti-bureaucratic antithesis of the role culture — coexists with the managerial culture in states five and six, both of which are represented in our sample, the fifth state by the second insurance broker and the sixth by the stores chain. Discriminant analysis has allowed us to state with some certainty that Harrison's pleasing descriptions correspond more nearly to dimensions than states, except where the other dimensions are not present. We found no cases of this in our research.

There is a better way of stating the problem. If Harrison's 'Task' and its converse 'Atomistic' were thought of as ideal types, achieved by means of playing roles or the exercise of power, we could think of his four cultures as:

(1) Task-achieved-by-role-play
(2) Task-achieved-by-power-play
(3) Personal gratification-achieved-by-role-play
(4) Personal gratification-achieved-by-power-play

Easier terms for this would be:

(1) Managerial – bureaucratic (manufacturing)
(2) Managerial – anti-bureaucratic (chain store)
(3) Ego-driven – bureaucratic (agency)
(4) Ego-driven – anti-bureaucratic (broking)

We can dispense, at last, with the terms centralization and formalization, which themselves are ideal types, better used for describing structures and functions than cultures. They do not help this analysis because, as we have seen from the Aston Data, organizations with different cultures may yet have the same structural determinants, and an ego-driven bureaucratic culture may be just as centralized and formalized as a managerial–bureaucratic culture. Thus it is not philosophically helpful to rely upon descriptions of the structure, function or decison-making processes to arrive at the culture. They are products of the culture not determinants of it. A leader in a managerial culture may decide to increase or decrease centralization in pursuit of task achievement, but in doing so he is not becoming more or less bureaucratic. In fact, as we saw, formalization is so closely related to size that he has fewer options on this score. Similarly the leaders of an ego-driven organization, where the dynamic of the firm is based upon the drives of its employees, may seek to harness their energies by ties of personal loyalty or by creating niches for them to work. In either case centralization or formalization are the means to the end and not the end itself.

We emerge from this exploration into the minds of other thinkers about organization culture stronger in the knowledge that the elements of culture can be derived from the characteristics of those who work in them — at senior levels. It is not simply a question of studying behaviour — attitudes and values of managers are equally important to an understanding of corporate culture.

6 The leader and the culture

Introduction

One of the questions arising out of the study of corporate culture is: why are we studying it at all? What has brought corporate culture into eminence as one of the key issues of the day? Is the concept an invention of anthropologically-minded academics to give themselves something to write about, much as the editor of a newspaper invents news during the summer silly season? Or have the events of the day brought a realization that organizations are more ephemeral than they used to be and that they need the 'glue' of corporate culture to hold them together? We believe that there is some weight in this argument. Since the technological explosion of the sixties and the belief that organization was the vehicle of technology rather than technology being the expression of organization, since the phenomenon of over-full employment enabled people to change jobs as easily as they changed their clothes, since access to capital markets made it easy to start organizations, and take them over, and since the improvement in communications enabled everyone to know everything in very short time-span, the organization as a way of life has been in decline. It has become unfashionable to acknowledge debts to patriarchalism, to be grateful to the leader for protection from the icy blasts of poor economic climates, or to recognize that the organization is as good as its leader. The social, political and economic universes have been dominated by weak leaders unable to use affluence or technology for the greater benefit of mankind, so that now in the eighties organizations are more difficult to lead than ever before because their leaders have fewer rewards or sanctions to offer their followers.

Moreover the rapid increase in the speed of development of technology has created a more serious human problem. Those in charge of organizations may no longer understand even the basic techniques employed within them. This is not grave in itself since the leaders of organizations are there to provide impetus towards new fields — their job is less to analyse than to comprehend, less to differentiate than to integrate. The essence of the crisis is that their immediate subordinates may not understand, still less communicate the desires of the field workers to the leader or the values of the leader to the field worker. This becomes particularly acute in the case of a change of leadership, or a change in the direction of the company. How is the leader to fashion an instrument capable of implementing his vision, or even capable of reacting positively to a change of plan, when the lines of communication are so attenuated, the noise-to-signal ratio so high? Hage and Dewar (1973) went even further: they argued that

> the values of the elite inner circle are more important than those of the executive director or of the entire staff in predicting innovation especially if the elite is defined behaviourally (those who participate in decision-making) rather than structurally (Executive Director and Departmental Heads) . . . These findings lend strong support to Thompson's (1967) notion that an inner circle does develop and it is their values that largely, though not completely, determine organizational policy. [pp. 287–8]

This is intuitively true, but difficult to test. In this study we prefer to think of the elite (those who have been sent for special, and hence normative, training) as the mediators of the culture. The chief executives believe themselves to play an important part in creating and changing culture, but as one of them remarked, the culture is what he *is*, not what he *wants*.

In this chapter we shall not be dealing with the whole complex question of leadership: others have done it better justice than could possibly be done here. In any case academics are in general ill-suited to making prescriptive statements about leadership, probably because intuition is difficult to analyze and leadership is an intuitive art. During our research we interviewed the leaders past and present of the organizations studied and now we set down, for the interest of the reader, some of their comments, under five headings.

The leader as culture-giver

Field Marshal Lord Montgomery is quoted as having said: 'I believe that one of the first duties of a military leader is to create what I call atmosphere.' So far as military atmosphere was concerned, this meant an atmosphere of optimistic determination to succeed, coupled with an attention to detail and a feeling of the inevitability of success. Montgomery, in many ways a shy man, went out of his way to make himself visible to his troops and communicate to them his own vision of the possibility of victory.

One of the chief executives, defining his job as 'to hold a rather difficult bunch of bloody-minded people together', amplified this statement as follows: 'I think the sort of people that I need here work better in a consensus-style atmosphere because they have to be capable of strong independent action and I really need to be somebody who holds them together rather than telling them precisely what to do . . . my job is to make the organization cohere.' Lord Nelson's message to his fleet on the eve of Trafalgar is significant in its vagueness ('England expects every man will do his duty'). Equally significant is Admiral Collingwood's reaction on receiving the message: 'Why does he keep sending us these messages: *we all know what to do*'.

The leader as epitome of behaviour

The business leader quoted above also explained the importance of setting standards of behaviour:

> If I operate on a basis of consensus other people tend to do the same thing: that is the expected style of the company. People who work for my subordinates would resent being dictated to if their bosses are not dictated to; it permeates through the organization . . . the junior managers know my style. They don't necessarily ape it but they do tend to conform to my ethos. If I was autocratic others might be very autocratic.

The style of the leader can never be ignored by the subordinates: some will exaggerate it, others may tend to rebel against it, but the style of the leader, both real and imagined, is as much a part of the culture as the technology or the rule-book.

The leader as the giver of meaning

One result of culture was, according to one leader, 'to give people a feeling of belonging'. This statement was amplified by another:

> All of us crave a sense of identity with what we do: this comes about by knowing what we are charged with doing and feeling part of an enterprise in which we can take pride. We want to work with people whom we can respect and we want other people to feel that we are making a contribution of value. It's a shorthand . . .

The leader as moderator of the culture

One of his tasks is to ensure that the organization is paying attention to all of its goals, both external and internal. Most of the chief executives interviewed had tried to change the culture, which had become inappropriate to the needs of the organization by the time they were appointed. It is interesting in this context to note how often the successor differed in character and style from his predecessor. In one cae it was possible to gather data about four generations of leadership. A likeable but indecisive leader, who coordinated but did not interfere with the efforts of able subordinates, provided the culture of expansionism necessary for a business struggling to make its mark in the marketplace. He was succeeded by one of those subordinates who consolidated the position and quadrupled the profitability of the organization in six years. He was highly effective although somewhat autocratic, preferring to direct the affairs of the company personally. After him came a more benevolent leader whose concern was to rebuild the corporate spirit. 'My task was maintaining morale and making sure that the feeling percolated down to the shop floor.' He gathered round him new able managers, many imported from other companies. His place has now been filled by another leader of outstanding intellectual calibre, with the task of giving prominence to new marketing techniques and better profitability. If the leader fails to read the culture he fails in his task.

This does not necessarily mean that the culture has collapsed. In one case a leader took over an organization whose cultures he described as 'healthy, but false'. His first task was to persuade his subordinates that their sometimes high-handed behaviour was not best suited to the aim of the organization. Another chief executive perceived his culture as 'honest but too conservative.' He set out to inspire his organization with the spirit of change. One leader saw the culture as directly related to the external environment: 'The culture might change if we were going downhill because there would be less consultation. In a growing business we can afford much more consultation.'

The leader as custodian of the culture

The leaders saw themselves as a product of their culture because with one exception they had risen from the lower ranks in the organization. In several cases the difficulty of changing the culture was mentioned. For example in the case of an organization that had to change its culture to survive, the leader commented: 'I have only partially succeeded in being identified with change . . . I perceive in myself some of the problems I have related . . .' In this sense the culture of the organization and the personality of the leader are closely interrelated. Yet culture need not be a constraint. Another said: 'It's amazing how almost everything we do here is based upon the value system of the founder of the firm; we are very much more conscious of this today than we were twenty years ago.' Given a certain value system the leader can make changes to the output by emphasizing some aspects of the business and de-emphasizing others, such as service rather than sales, or employee concern rather than profits. 'Every chief executive runs the business through one side of it.'

Such musings may give the impression that the leaders interviewed were somewhat withdrawn and given to introspection; and this is probably true. One of the chief misapprehensions generated by the literature on leadership is that the leader is an outgoing, clubbable sort of person, much given to backslapping and hearty pursuits. The reality is otherwise. Each of the leaders interviewed was sensitive to nuance. Many said it was a lonely job. This may have been due to the indivisibility of ultimate responsibility but was also a necessary virtue in that it enabled all kinds of subordinates to relate to the qualities they chose to perceive in their boss, just as, to use Isobel Briggs Myers' metaphor, the introvert leader remains in his campaign tent whilst his extrovert subordinate transmits information to him and orders from him, so the business leader operates through, rather than on, his surroundings.

The leader then is faced with a dilemma. The culture gives him his power over the organization. Yet the culture may ascribe to him the wrong sort of power for the achievement of changes necessary to keep the organization in peak condition. It may want him to be wise, when there is nothing to be wise about. It may want him to preserve when there is nothing worth preserving. The leader, like the hymn-writer, sees change and decay in all around. Leaders of organizations are faced with the risk that by changing techniques, methods and people they may destroy the delicate tissue that makes their organization unique, gives employees their sense of identity and enables them to move crabwise from an empty rock-pool to one where the pickings are better, without disconnecting the stabilizing values and attitudes from human behaviour and thus losing control of the machine they operate, and which operates them. On the other hand it is often quite plain that the existing path leads only to disaster.

Thus the leader has a complex relationship with the culture. He has to ensure that it is well defined, meets the needs of the organization, enables him to keep the ethos of the organization and yet is sufficiently flexible for him to change the path of the organization without so disrupting the culture that it fails to provide recognizable codes of practice. This creates a heavy burden for the conscientious leader because he has to recognize that the culture, if it becomes an extension of his personality, becomes an extension of his own shortcomings. To recognize parts of yourself that are counter-productive and alter the culture to make allowances for this is as easy as designing a strait-jacket and sewing yourself into it. It is difficult to believe that the end justifies the means; yet it must be done if the culture is to survive the shortcomings of the leader.

Conclusion

We have tried in this short chapter to give a flavour of the preoccupation of the leaders we interviewed with the problem of culture. For reasons of confidentiality it has not been possible to reproduce in anything like the rich detail the interviews that took place. But they do confirm that culture is not a concept invented by academics to increase the number of their publications. Whether it is called 'atmosphere', 'company spirit' or 'ethos', it is part of the tissue of organizational life and would deserve to be studied if only as a phenomenon of leadership. Yet, as we have seen, it is more than a tool with which leaders attempt to manipulate employees. It is the expression of the sense of identity of those who have made common cause within the confines of a set of objectives and a market place.

The aim of this chapter has been to recount the reactions of chief executives from five different organizations to the same stimulus. The differences between their replies (given the common belief that in some way they influenced the culture of their organizations) indicates how far they have been influenced by the working conditions in which they found themselves; the need to respond to a felt challenge, on the part of their subordinates and their predecessors; to enact the organization culture in a different yet recognizable way, within the character of the organization. Each of them would have been capable, one feels, of doing the job of the other. But the words used to describe the organizational ideas and the ideas themselves arise from their organizational experience. The writer believes that in a very literal sense the chief executive is the mouthpiece of the organization — expressing it to the outside world, and to itself. The organization has two voices, as some have noticed — the inner and the outer. And in the chief executive these speak together. Perhaps they over-rate their own importance as creators or moderators of culture, but as one of them explained, the ability to improve the lives of others is what gives the job its savour. Without it there would be little else to compensate for the burden of office.

7 Changing the culture

Introduction

Organizations in transition are not a pretty sight. When some stimulus — internal or more often external — causes them to change direction the atmosphere becomes thick with confusion and morale falls. Employees lose pride in their work and in the success of the organization. Commitment disappears in a welter of recrimination about what ought to happen. People refuse to cooperate either with one another or their leaders. Redundancy programmes and sudden promotions are viewed with equal mistrust. And in the midst of all this trauma, the customer finds himself enjoying a low priority in the scheme of things and often departs, if he can, to find a better welcome elsewhere, at least until the tumult and shouting have died.

No one so far as we know has written a book or chapter entitled: 'Organization Change Can Be Fun', although academic bookshelves are full of more or less prescriptive treatises on the subject, and this is hardly to be wondered at: for every person in the organization gaining from the change, five or six stand to lose. No wonder that organization leaders, faced with the need for change, just do it and hope for the best. Other courses are long, hard and may be unsuccessful. In any case consultation seems to undermine the prerogative of the 'father' to decide what is best for the 'family' and thus further prolong the period when the ship is 'in irons', its sails flapping aimlessly in the wind. Finally the ship sets off on its new tack, the crew take up new stations and, hopefully, the obstacles are successfully negotiated and new progress is made. Sometimes, alas, the progress is in the wrong direction and after a period, usually about five years, of further unrest, a fresh upheaval becomes necessary to avert a fresh set of possible disasters. Lest it be thought that the writer is making a mountain out of a molehill, here are a couple of examples.

The first concerns a port operating authority whose board decided that in view of changes in the economic climate, the technology and working conditions (notably the decasualization of labour), it was necessary to redesign the organization (for a full account see Graves (1976)). The structure was duly revamped to include several profit centres and the accompanying information and personnel performance systems were installed. Delighted with their work, organization leaders and consultants stood back and awaited a dramatic change in the fortunes of the authority. It soon came, but in the wrong direction. Operating costs went sky-high, morale crashed to rock bottom and invisible hatches between the layers of management slammed shut with almost audible clangs. Other consultants brought in to study the break-down in communications could only point to the divorce between aspiration and reality. A change in the goals of the organization engineered by top management corresponded neither to real possibilities, nor to custom and practice, nor to the values of the employees down the line. The strong culture of the dock operators (known by them as dockology) was undermined and nothing put in its place. The middle management could not understand, still less operate, the new organization and before long it lapsed into empty bureaucracy, each person seeking his own advantage, to the detriment of the company as a whole. Peace was only restored when the last of the 'Old Guard' departed leaving the 'Young Turks' in possession of the field. In this case it might have been better to arrange this from the start. Unfortunately the Young Turks did not understand how to work ships.

A second example concerns a firm in the construction industry whose autocratic founder retired from the chair, but not from the board, at a great age and proceeded to install in his place first one, then a second faithful subordinate, both past retirement age. The first was content to leave the organization as it had been, but the second presided over wholesale decentralization into profit centres. The result was the same: spiralling overheads, loss of cutting edge and a dramatic increase in losses caused by lack of control. After the departure of the second ex-subordinate, the company had to be reorientated and the damage done to the culture will probably take years to purge.

These examples are taken from large organizations; one might expect the problem to be attenuated in small ones. But this is not so. Small organizations are more vunerable than large ones. They are more prone to takeover (especially if successful); they cannot offer their staff such interesting careers, nor pay them so much. It is often impossible to design clear charts because one person may be doing two or three different jobs (this is especially true in the field of insurance broking where the producer of the business may have to broke the risk and even deal with the claim). In small organizations (less than 300 people) the chief executive may also be, to all intents and purposes, the proprietor. Having arranged the organization for his own convenience and created the culture in his own image, he is likely to know little and care less about succession or market niches. The organization ambles on until he retires and dies and the 'deluge' arrives.

Changing the culture: some ideas

Is there an easy solution? Solution, yes; easy, no. It consists first in recognizing the culture and analysing its causes — the technology, the leadership, the markets — then in deciding how far the culture is appropriate to the current situation in which the organization finds itself. These are the two steps with which we have been mainly concerned in this book. The third step is to change the culture itself, without destroying it. There are three levels at which this can take place:

Changing of behaviour only

At this level we are not seeking to change people's attitudes or values but to modify their behaviour. This can usually be effected by training followed by the installation of some type of performance monitoring device such as an information system or performance review. It will cause people to work faster (or slower); to communicate better (or worse); to economize on the use of resources (or squander them more). But whatever the change, it takes place without any basic alteration to attitudes to work or values about work. Changes such as this can often be wrought by indirect means such as rearrangement of offices, repainting, redesign of agendas for meetings to bring different subjects into prominence, re-timing of meetings, even redesign of notepaper and forms. An exhibition firm actually uses different notepaper for each exhibition it runs and this highlights the uniqueness of each exhibition. As a result employees pay attention to different aspects of each exhibition and even the data about it. However, the general attitude of employees to exhibition production is not affected. In another firm the chief executive has installed a personal computer in his office to encourage others to do likewise. Safety awards, suggestion schemes and other direct incentive schemes may well change behaviour without affecting attitudes. It is important however in each case to stress to employees that the attitudes and values remain the same — in order to forestall doubts and questions. This is easier where firms have a clearly spelt out ideology, such as exist in IBM and Marks and Spencer (both family-based cultures).

Changing attitudes

Employee attitudes are based upon the perceived behaviour of the high priests of the culture, as shown in Chapter Six in the discussion on the role of the chief executive in determining culture. If the departmental head cares more for technical excellence of the product than sales turnover, then so will his cohorts. To change the attitudes of these people certainly requires some adjustment of their mental set and may require structural readjustment to give greater prominence to some departments at the expense of others. In the port operating authority the rise in the importance of the accounting department, the creation of a marketing department and the dissolution of the engineering department did much to change attitudes towards the customer. Unfortunately it was not explained that these changes were intended to improve the efficiency of the port without detroying its value system and the operation was seen in terms of gains and losses in interdepartmental 'wars of the roses'. In this case not only were people required to change their reporting system but the organization found itself having to cope with an influx of people from outside the company, bringing with them different values. Conversely, in another organization, the hiring of a succession of computer experts without any attempt to change attitudes to Electronic Data Processing did nothing to improve attitudes towards computerization. In this organization the culture required a new entrant to construct his own power base. The business-getters (termed 'hunters') had the upper hand, while the administrative staff (the 'housekeepers') were seen, by virtue of their status and reward packages, to be of lesser importance. Attitudes are not changed by exhortation but by explanation. In this case it required a board level appointment of an administrator to change the attitudes of the employees towards EDP.

Changing values

The chief executive of one of our firms was in retrospect dissatisfied with his ability to motivate others, and attributed this to failure to 'initiate, delegate and supervise, which is what I believe one is supposed to do'. As a result the commercial success that he brought to the company was soon eroded. 'When he retired we were losing ground because we had no management skill.' He blamed himself for this failure to impart lasting change to the culture. His three terms, plucked out of the air (or more precisely his memory) are significant for our purpose. They remind us of the findings of factor analysis which showed that there are three sorts of manager with quite different personal characteristics. An intellectual, this manager had surrounded himself with subordinates who were good 'supervisors' or 'initiators' but poor delegators. When he retired there was no one to step into his role.

This example leads us to the somewhat radical conclusion that if you want to change the value system you have to change the people at the top, whose value system permeates the culture. In the case of a construction company the new chief executive has spent much time and energy in promoting a new value code. Furthermore he is taking steps to ensure that those around him combine all the skills of initiating, supervising and delegating and are not simply carbon copies of himself. Thus his task becomes, in a real sense, 'holding a rather difficult bunch of bloody-minded people together'. For as Belbin (1981) and others have shown, the most effective teams combine people who do not necessarily get on well together. Indeed this was shown to be the case when the board of one organization completed Ghiselli inventories. Each one was easily identifiable as a 'fixer', 'supervisor' or 'consultant'.

Does this always mean importing managers at the top level? If you seek continuous high performance, the answer regrettably is usually 'yes'. Those who have achieved promotion to the board from within have to be recognized. At junior levels this means being a good 'fixer' — displaying initiative, resourcefulness, self-confidence and conforming to the culture. At middle level they earn recognition by their ability to supervise others — get things done, achieve targets set by others — and conforming to the culture. The 'consultants' among them, those with the capacity to think, plan, do research on new markets, seek out new ideas, are often seen as insubordinate, deviant or simply uncommitted. They do not fit easily into the organizational cultural model and are not seen as conforming to the culture; so they become the odd men out, and do not rise in the ranks. Consequently when the chief executive looks round to find someone with fresh ideas, there are no obvious candidates. He is forced either to promote a youngster over many heads, or look outside. If he has not the stomach for the former course and the latter search proves fruitless, the organization can only continue on the previous tack, its path diverging increasingly from the market. Research and development becomes an end in itself rather than a means to renovation of the culture.

Effecting the change

So much for the essential question. The remaining problem is how to do it. In our study of a reinsurance broker (1981), we tried to demonstrate that there is a sequence of events that enables culture to be changed without too much cultural disturbance of the kind we mentioned at the beginning of this chapter. It consists of an interactive process of dialogue between inaugurators and those affected. In the case we cited there the problem was to unite two cultures and the solution was to create a new culture with characteristics of both the parents — a type of corporate progeniture if one can call it that. This was done in classic style by uniting both sides to cope with an external threat — a natural disaster that rocked the market — and an internal problem, that of moving to new premises. Specifically, in creating the new organization the chief executive took pains to break down enclaves of ex-'Drake' or ex-'Cecil' employees. In other organizations where this is not done problems of non-cooperation and inter-departmental conflict soon arise.

Having conquered the first problem — that of merging the two cultures — the chief executive was faced with a second: how to improve the managerialism of the organization? Hitherto, in common with other broking firms, the employees rated business-getting high and business administration low. Now it became important to secure better coordination between the departments and specifically between producer-brokers and administrators. Helped by his previous experience he decided to hold a kind of committee of enquiry. At the preliminary meeting of the committee, which consisted of the senior directors, it was clear that opinions were divided over both the need for change and the method to be adopted. Some argued that no change in values was necessary, just greater energy in the prosecution of business. Any change in attitudes would upset the clients and reduce the efficiency of the firm. They favoured change in behaviour only.

Others favoured a change in attitude but enforced from board level. Life was too short to engage in a lengthy process of consultation during which dirty linen might be aired. Whichever strategy was adopted, whether change or status quo, some people, disappointed that their arguments had not carried the day, would be de-motivated and would not be committed to making the solution work. Still others thought the chief executive would lose his personal authority in appearing not to be omniscient. However in the end the chief executive (who was also the chairman) prevailed upon his board to give the process a trial, on three conditions: first he reserved the right not to accept the verdict of the majority of those who gave evidence; second, only written evidence would be accepted, amplified if necessary by testimony; and third, the process was not to take more than three months. These conditions being accepted, an invitation was issued to all members of the firm from supervisor level upwards (about sixty people) to submit their views on how the image and profitability of the firm could be improved.

Twenty-three papers were received, including those from board members. Those interviewed included several from the most junior levels of supervision, many of whom were relatively recent recruits. Each paper was first discussed by the committee and then the author was invited to state his views and answer questions. During the hearings, which took place about once a week over four weeks, a remarkable change came over the members of the committee. Interest began to focus not upon whether the paper supported or did not support the particular member's view, but whether the arguments in the paper were well presented and cogent. At the outset each departmental head was looking to see whether his subordinate was toeing the party line. By the end of the hearing (when everyone knew what each departmental line was) the 'dissidents' aroused more interest than the 'conformists'. Once again the chief executive had been able to swing the focus away from personal problems towards the development of the culture.

By the end of the committee of inquiry the answer seemed a foregone conclusion: more responsibility should be given to the field workers and the accent moved from functionalism to geographical areas of activity. The chief executive now had a different problem: to curb the committee's enthusiasm for radical change. Logic had pointed the way, but instinct still hung back.

In order to work through this problem he called a one-day seminar of all the directors to discuss the findings. At this seminar much of the enthusiasm for change evaporated before the reality that some directors would have fewer responsibilities while others would see their jobs become still more onerous. After a long and at times heated discussion it was agreed to give the new structure a limited trial in one department only, deferring for a year the final decision. Fears were expressed about the severely increased cost in staff, about changes in layout of the offices, about the incompetence of staff to handle their new responsibilities, about unfair divisions of labour (and rewards).

However the change was duly implemented. Twelve months later a review meeting was held to assess the value of the reorganization, and a remarkable change in the culture was apparent. The middle management, who had hitherto sought to emulate the rather understated approach to management problems, had now become much more pro-active. Instead of seeking guidance from their senior directors, they sought to guide *them* towards a more professional approach. Naturally this did not elicit whole-hearted approval from those who thought that age and experience confer wisdom. However it was noticeable that by the end of the conference those who understood the process of management best were listened to — because of force of argument, not personality. It was as if the members of the conference now saw their own strengths and weaknesses in better perspective. As a result of this whole process the culture of the organization, which at the time of the research was a patriarchal culture, has probably moved more in the direction of managerialism.

Many problems have yet to be ironed out, such as negative attitudes to performance review, integrated data processing, performance targets and promotion and pay criteria, which were a standard part of the old culture. The significant aspect of this case is the trouble taken by the chief executive to change the culture organically in order to take his 'bloody-minded bunch of subordinates' with him. For in a small firm such as this is, passengers cannot be afforded. However 'bloody-minded' they may seem, all the directors make an important contribution to the profitability of the firm; to lose the commitment of even one would do calculable and significant damage. What the chief executive did achieve was a change in attitude without changing the written-down ideology of the firm, which incidentally forms the subject of the first session in training pro-grammes. It should also be remembered that this event took place in a highly successful firm whose profits had doubled in five years. In firms facing recession a cultural change is just as important but then the chief executive may have to act more pro-actively. However it would seem that the stages of consultation and limited implementation are still an essential part of the creation of commitment.

Choosing the culture

We come finally to the most important part of this chapter: which culture do we want for our firm, and what adjustments do we make to the existing cultural mix? For an answer, we turn once again to our original analysis. It will be remembered that discriminant analysis has revealed three dimensions:

— the managerial versus the egocentric
— the bureaucratic versus the anti-bureaucratic
— the problem-solving versus the non-problem-solving.

For ease of discussion we will call this third dimension simply pro-active (looking for problems to solve) and reactive (dealing with problems as they arise). These dimensions, although they could theoretically describe a culture, rarely do so in practice and we need to think of them in combinations.

For further ease of discussion we will follow Harrison in giving the cultures labels: but we have indicated that Harrison's names seem to indicate the pure forms and are based upon theory rather than research. The notion of raising them to the level of theologies (see Handy (1978)), while appealing, does nothing to validate them, although the success of his book does show that managers feel there is a theological (or mythological) aspect to culture. Furthermore, we shall try to show that there is no ideal culture. Those who have used Harrison's cultural types when working with managers have found (as he did) that managers usually choose, as the culture they would like to work in, the Task type (corresponding to the 'Consulting' management style). Our culture types are not intended to be normative in this way: each culture can be right for a firm seeking success.

Figure 7.1 shows the names of the cultures we have observed in the research. They relate to the different kind of social structure we have seen.

Barbarian

This describes an anti-bureaucratic, ego-driven culture where there is conscious rejection of procedures and formality. Indeed it is seen as a symbol of success in a barbarian culture that certain members of it are 'above the law'. These 'warriors' have enormous expense accounts, keep whatever hours they please and do not have to justify

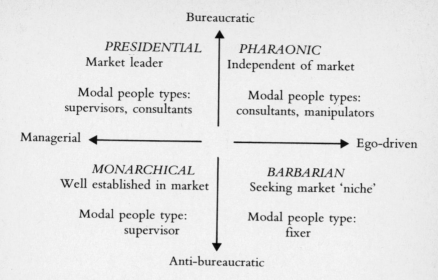

Figure 7.1 *Four cultures*

through the 'normal channels' requests for resources. In return for this special treatment the successful barbarian will create business for his organization where none existed. He will work hours that would kill off a more ordered individual and so he achieves his successes at the cost of ill-health and broken marriages. This is the culture for the workaholic, the maverick, the pop-star. The style of leadership is purely charismatic in the sense that there is no rationality about it. In fact leadership style is relatively unimportant because the organization consists only of unstable groups which probably alter from task to task. It is usually recognizable by its quirky premises — either spread over a number of seedy converted houses or architect-designed in leather and satin-finished steel.

In a barbarian culture there is an air of perpetual ferment, as if something earth-shattering (either for its clients or its employees) is always about to happen. There is always secrecy about its operations, since surprise is the hallmark of its activities, and its successes and failures are confused by the tides of fulsome praise and harsh criticism that flow alternately over the various happenings. The leader of a barbarian organization holds sway through a mixture of terror and charm. The mythology that spreads about him is of his unpredictability, his meanness punctuated with wild flashes of generosity and his own inordinate powers be they physical, mental or merely financial. It is the organization where people wear their hangovers like rotary badges. To work in organizations such as these, living off the land with the occasional share of booty, is to experience the thrill of the switchback, the euphoria of high life and occasionally the bitterness of despair. Perhaps the most obvious example is the advertising agency.

So far as character type is concerned, the modal type may be expected to be 'fixers', strong in battle, truculent in defeat and contemptuous of the settled life. This is precisely what leads such organizations to seek a more ordered way of existence, and in the end they seek to create a more ordered culture, such as the one we next describe.

Monarchical

The first difference to note about the monarchical culture is that the chief person claims to rule by force of law, rather than through naked power. In practice it may come to the same thing because the king's activities can rarely be questioned and even then only indirectly. However in this culture as opposed to the barbarian culture, the army is paid on a (more or less) regular basis and the senior officers have different uniforms from the NCOs. In the monarchical culture there is still a good deal of contempt for formalization and bureaucracy, and little tendency to spend time on such organizational fripperies as planning and market research. On the other hand each person knows what it is he or she has to do and virtues of loyalty and doggedness are highly praised and priced. The long service badge is less a nostalgic souvenir than a seal of approval, a symbol of acceptance into the brotherhood, and there are secret signs and rituals to match.

Such an organization culture is heavily dependent upon the character and ability of its king: if he is weak the organization is at risk because it still reflects his personality to a critical extent. Two other features of monarchy affect this culture: mortality and succession. In a laudable attempt to maintain security, leaders of monarchical organizations often overstay their time and act as a brake on innovation. Early attempts to clarify the line of succession will, if successful, impoverish the ranks of the 'lieutenants', the more talented of whom, seeing their way to the top barred, will seek office elsewhere, leaving the second-rate, unimaginative and trusty foot sloggers. This is why, in monarchical organizations where promotion comes from within, the quality of the leadership is so variable. For the leadership of such organizations requires flair and intelligence — qualities not bred (nor even perhaps tolerated) by the organization. The model character types for this culture are 'fixers' and 'supervisors'. Any 'consultants' keep their skills well hidden, if they wish to remain in contention.

Presidential

The 'barbarian' and 'monarchical' cultures are to be found in some of our most successful businesses, but because of the personality impact of the leader they are likely to be limited in size (although this is by no means always the case). The third culture that we have observed is called 'presidential' because of the influence to be found within it of democracy, status and coordination. In presidential cultures the elected leader embodies, for the time of his office (usually not more than ten years) the needs and aspirations of the people. Careers are easy to make and real rewards are available for those displaying outstanding talents. There is an open acceptance of the system as the way to triumph over the incapacities of the person (the writer was once told by a French chief executive that the proof of the superiority of the Roman Catholic Church over all other sects was that it had survived the inadequacies of its priesthood). Just as the American presidents have reflected the virtues, aspirations and occasionally frailties of their culture, so presidents of business organizations reflect and validate the current preoccupations within that culture. The leader is sustained in office by subordinates who know his term is short and thus his influence limited. Deference is exaggerated by the knowledge that the genuflexion is to the podium, not its occupant. Whatever his ability, he remains 'Mr President'.

The problem with such a culture is that it is confusing, calling for clear messages from the leadership if it is not to drift into a superfluity of by-ways. Its very complexity militates against clarity and the writer worked with one presidential organization where three sub-cultures and three types of organization structure were vying for pre-eminence. The president's strategy seemed to be: let them vie! Such divide-and-rule tactics are heavily consumptive of energy but the apparent tolerance of such internal competition probably springs more from the president's lack of freedom to manoeuvre than his machiavellian desire to see the sub-parts of his culture destroy one another. Maybe even he must see to it that the sub-cultures remain alive so that he can move his whole organization in one cultural direction or another as the need arises. It is with presidential cultures that problems of pro-activity and reactivity become most acute. First, there is the question of coordination. How can one combine in one culture the virtues of those who achieve their results by managing resources with those whose greatest satisfaction derives from the operation of a system? Unless the goals are clearly spelt out and accepted, both types of person — the supervisors and the consultants — will be efficient but not effective, their combined efforts cancelling each other out. Without a president prepared to seek new problems, the whole organization lives on its internal momentum, and the end, when it comes, is as unexpected as the size of the disaster. It is hard to keep each of the elements alive in the culture, but where this is achieved the culture breeds success, as in the case of IBM, though sometimes at the expense of the personal identity and autonomy of its members.

Pharaonic

Like that of the ancient Egyptians this culture is hard to appreciate if you have not experienced it, yet it is every whit as attractive (and at times frustrating) as the other three. The two main dimensions of the culture are the pre-eminence of the system and the individualism of its members. Any visitor to the temples and tombs of the pharaonic Egyptians is struck by the respect, amounting to passion, for order, status and ritual. It informs and inspires every sculpture, every painting, every architectural plan. This does not lead to the dull monochrome we call bureaucracy: on the contrary, paintings, decorations and architecture all stress lightness — black is only used for drawing eyes and outlines — grey not at all. The god is basically a sun-god but tempered by the quality of the unknowable that leads to the need for interpretation and order so strong that an attempt by a later Egyptian Pharaoh Akenaten to restore the directness and simplicity of sun-worship was defeated by his own high priests, presumably with the support of his own people. A culture such as this favours the creative arts, personal growth, the organization and husbandry of resources but not the education of people to work in organized stable groups. Organizations with the pharaonic culture are changeless, yet shadowy, or as the leader of the government agency put it: healthy, but false. A pro-active pharaonic organization will seek for situations where its ability to create law and order are useful in stabilizing a fluid market. A reactive pharaonic organization seeks merely to perpetuate the glories of the past, adjusted if possible so as to be of relevance to the present. Its leaders are people capable of tolerating the endless monotony of ritual, while yet maintaining a spark of individualism sufficient to enable those lower down in the hierarchy to relate to them, to say of them: 'He goes through the motions, but he may not believe in it any more than I do: in his bondage he is free, and so am I.' In a purely pharaonic culture we might expect to find the modal personality characteristics of the consultant and the manipulator (this character was only found in the government agency) — the supervisor being superseded by the system. However in our example there were many supervisors, probably needed to achieve the objectives of the organization in spite of its bureaucratic structure. At all events, no one questioned the necessity for formality, and its failure to provide answers to questions was condoned, for this was a reactive pharaonic culture.

The Relationship Between the Four Cultures

In devising these titles for the four culture types we have observed, it may be thought that there is a certain sense of historical evolution in the way organization cultures develop, and we believe that this is generally so. The cultures of new (or newly amalgamated) organizations are often 'barbarian' because it is their animal dynamism that secures them a place in the market at the outset and they have to fight hard to survive. But it is an unstable form, more suited to winning business than retaining it. Sooner or later organizations such as our second insurance broker decide to modify their culture to something more permanent — seeking to secure immortality for the organization if not for the leader. At this stage an element of order creeps in, people begin to be respected for their ability to manage on their own, and they also become aware of the possibility of creating their own kingdoms within the kingdom, sometimes, like the medieval coinage, in the king's name, sometimes in their own.

The principle of absolute authority is, however, irksome to the masses and sooner or later if the people are strong, they will tame the monarch and reduce him to the status of principal agent. In such cases he may well feel himself trapped in a system that he fails to understand at his peril. He has to succeed at two examinations — and be capable of governing as well as presiding (or reigning!).

There seems however to be a Gresham's Law of culture which causes respect for the system to drive out respect for the group, and thus leads to our pharaonic category, where cohesion is sacrificed on the altar of order. In the end the pharaonic civilization foundered upon intolerance. The individual went his own way independently of the need to cooperate; and this failure brought disaster and barbarism!

This model should provide insights into appropriate organization cultures. A presidential culture is more appropriate to complex tasks than a barbarian culture and a pharaonic culture is more suitable to publicly elected bodies than a monarchical one — for its official structure at least. The model also shows that different types of people inhabit the cultures and are comfortable within them, and how an absence of one or other of the three types can represent a danger to its own continuation.

We are thus brought back to the most fundamental questions: weak culture or strong? Right culture or wrong? To the first question the answer comes unanimously from the chief executives interviewed: it is essential, for business success, that the culture should be strong — that people within the organization should recognize and if possible adopt the values and attitudes espoused by the leader and high priests. They will certainly have to adopt their behaviour patterns should they wish to be successful. We were able to find no case where the culture was weak, as measured by the discriminant analysis technique, but the business successful.

However there were cases where the culture was strong but the business was unsuccessful. This was because the culture was inappropriate to the aims of the business. One of the cultures we encountered was strongly barbarian: the people in it were individually competent, capable, hardworking and motivated, but collectively they were failing to realize the organization's potential. That this has been changed is due to the leader's determination to change the culture. Similarly, we encountered an organization with a strongly monarchical culture but at the time of the research the organization was unfortunate in having to undertake a remodelling of its cadre to include a larger number of 'consultants', a type filtered out by the previous regime. In due course this organization may move more towards the presidential mode, but this is unlikely as the sector in which it operates requires a king who is able to take rapid decisions 'in the field' rather than a 'capitol', which may seek to determine policy for eventualities that cannot be foreseen. In addition it is difficult to achieve a strong presidential culture, it is too easy to lose sight of corporate values unless they are continually reinforced.

The choice of the first three cultures we have described is also much affected by economic questions: unless the margins allow it, a strong culture of monarchy (which implies something to hand on to future kings), or presidency (which implies a well developed value system) are unlikely to be built up. The cultures of Egypt and Barbary are relatively simple to create because they appeal to mankind at an instinctive level (self-preservation) and for all that are relatively durable.

Conclusion

Is culture then an optional extra, an ill-afforded luxury or add-on? We believe not. People go to work to find meaning in their lives — to belong to the horde, the kingdom, the democracy, the cult. Work organizations and those that direct their affairs have a basic obligation to provide a satisfaction of that need, in fact, for many an organization the culture is its only distinguishing feature. If we are honest with ourselves we would rather live under barbarian rule than under no rule at all. The larger an organization grows, the more it becomes necessary to work at reinforcing and regenerating the culture, modifying it here and there to take account of the values and attitudes of those who have entered the organization but who are not yet the culture-makers.

The expansionist age of the sixties, which broke so many of the fetters of civilization, has created a generation of people for whom ego needs are more important than needs to belong. The educational emphasis was upon non-conformism, upon rejection of authority, upon 'doing your own thing'. In the eighties, with high unemployment the spectre haunting our society and threatening to demolish it, the national solution has been to encourage people to start up small businesses, to begin again, to become the 'barbarians' of the future. According to our diagram this makes good sense, but it is bound to pose questions about the proactiveness of large organizations. Faced with the impossibility of recruiting conformists, will they restructure themselves to admit mavericks: will the Presidents become Pharaohs?

Finally we should not lull ourselves into believing that corporate culture can be neatly divided into eight segments. Nobody, with the possible exception of the author in his more manic moments, can believe that. Although our scientific understanding of things is reasonably sophisticated, our scientific comprehension of people is surprisingly rudimentary. We seem to fear pigeonholes for people, at the same level as we detest genetic experiment.

Our conclusions are therefore speculative: we have been trying to create a frame of mind conducive to more scientific attempts to analyse the complexities of human behaviour with the rudimentary tools at our disposal.

8 The next step

Summary of the research

At this point it is perhaps useful to remind the reader of some of the key findings in the research, in order that future seekers after truth may be aware of some of the new ground to be covered.

A review of the literature uncovered two basically different approaches to the problem of organization culture. It was shown that the anthropological approach treated culture as a phenomenon in its own right, whereas the psycho-social approach treated culture (usually called 'climate') as a variable capable of manipulation by management so as to improve productivity and performance. Since the tools used by the latter borrowed heavily from job satisfaction questionnaires it was concluded that the subjective nature of the enquiry was more likely to yield soft data (social facts) than hard comparable data. Structuralists such as Payne and Pugh came to the conclusion that individual characteristics such as personality and intellectual ability had an important influence on perceptions of the meanings attributed to organizational culture. It was, as Guion concluded, more an attribute of people than of organizations. Culture was in this sense, to quote Evan (1968) a multi-dimensional perception of the essential attributes or character of an organizational system. The crucial question was therefore the identification and measurement of generalized and shared orientations of individuals, together with a study of the sources of such patterns and the processes of their aquisition by individuals and their effects on individual and organizational behaviour.

The purpose of this research was, therefore, to investigate the extent to which certain characteristics of key managers in selected and contrasting work organizations were consistently patterned. Organizations were chosen where the researcher could test questionnaire data and its interpretations against other more qualitative information of historical development, etc. The personal characteristics of some of the senior management who attended in-house, off-site courses at the Management Centre could thus be compared with the history of the development of the organizations, the attitudes and values of the leaders of those organizations and the behaviour of those organizations in setting up training courses.

In the study of the training programmes it was much easier to make comparisons and these immediately threw into relief differences in behaviour between organizations in such matters as authorization of training expenditure, monitoring and evaluating behaviour, involvement of the personnel director and the effect of the training as perceived by the companies. For example, in the agency the main result achieved was seen to be better integration of participants, whereas in private companies the training was seen to improve awareness. In the manufacturing company the output of one training programme affected decisions about the input of the next, implying that management regarded benefits to the system as more important than benefits to the individual.

The interviews with corporate leaders were revealing in the light of the generally high importance attached to the concept of culture by these men. Whether in view of their position they felt more aware of its presence as they tried to adapt it to suit the changing needs of the market place, or whether they saw the concept as a means of ensuring compliance and predictability on the part of their subordinates is not certain. However, they all agreed that a strong culture was necessary for a successful business. Significantly, they also agreed that they had made attempts to change the culture since coming into office. They all thought that one of the most significant determinants of corporate culture was the management style of the chief executive, and this also leads to the conclusion that, except in family controlled businesses, the organizational culture is only as permanent as the collective memory of the chief executive who most profoundly affected the business, simply because different people pay attention to different aspects of the business, be they control systems, new developments or different approaches to the market. The interviews were also remarkable for the difference of the vocabularies used: for instance, the 'bureaucratic' leader was more precise and objective than the 'managerial' leader. A study of

language used may well be as valuable in the analysis of
organizational culture as it has been in the analysis of national
culture.

Chapter Four set out the conclusions from the analysis of data
available from the protocols of 612 managers of which about half
(322) worked at senior levels in the organizations studied. Each of the
sub-samples contained at least thirty managers. The first task was to
validate the research tool and it was demonstrated that where there
were two levels of seniority within the sub-sample the characteristics
of the more senior managers varied in the direction predicted by
Ghiselli. This seems to demonstrate that although the research tool
was not primarily designed for British managers, it was at least
reliable as a measuring device, and the factor analysis loadings were
quite similar for the first factor to those Ghiselli had obtained.

Ghiselli had, however, restricted his data analysis to ordinary
factor analysis. The second task of the research was to try to refine
the analysis of individual managers in the whole sample to locate
basic types of managerial orientation. By using the Varimax method,
in which the axes are rotated to obtain more significant loadings on
the second and ensuing factors, it became apparent that there are
three types of manager commonly encountered in the survey: the
'fixers' (loading heavily on initiative and low need for reward); the
'supervisors' (loading heavily on need for self-actualization and low
need for security) and the 'consultants' (loading heavily on
intelligence, self-assurance and need for achievement). The variance
accounted for by these three factors differed from one organization
to another, but it was surmised that 'fixers' are managers successful at
junior and middle level, and maybe in staff functions, whereas
'supervisors' are managers who succeed at jobs requiring the co-
ordination of many people and 'consultants' are those managers
whose jobs include a high degree of conceptualization. These three
stereotypes gleaned from the Varimax factors found reassuring
support from the literature on managerial roles and decision-
making, an indication that the managerial role is divisible into three
statistically observable sections. These findings have consequences
for selection and training methods as well as for corporate culture
research.

The main statistical analysis in Chapter Four however, was

concerned with the identification of dimensions of organization culture directly from the personal data in the sample. Several interesting findings emerged. First, it was possible to discriminate between service and manufacturing firms on the data alone. Secondly, it was found that there were three main dimensions of organization culture: administrative, managerial and problem-solving. Using these three functions it was possible not only to identify each company separately, but also to show that companies in similar industries had cultures that showed a similar profile on these dimensions. Furthermore, a dynamic was introduced into the model: that of 'acculturation'. The insurance broker which, by reason of recent mergers, has not yet developed a strong individual culture, was shown, by this model, to be a-cultural. The manufacturing company had a managing and administrative and problem-solving culture, whereas the agency was primarily administrative. These three dimensions also belonged to the literature of corporate culture, but this is perhaps the first occasion on which the model was derived solely from personal characteristics of senior organization employees. The most popular model previously cited, that of Harrison, which was shown to be basically related to the structural dimensions of centralization and formalization, now seemed inadequate as an alternative means of categorizing organizational culture.

In Chapter Seven some attempt was made to test how far the Aston Group's data set provided a good explanation of the differing forms of organizational structure. It was hoped to use this data as independent evidence of the importance of organizational contexts in determining the viability of different forms of culture. Despite some hopeful indications concerning relationships with external agents such as suppliers, clients and trade unions, the analysis yielded rather little of significance, apart from confirmation that, first, organizations in the service sector seem to operate according to a different set of rules to those in the manufacturing sector — perhaps to do with the decentralization of decision-making; and second, that public sector organizations tend to be more centralized and formalized than those in the private sector, that is to say they are more administratively biased. There was some indication that the Harrison model has a dynamic element caused by increases in size, for in the private sector it was the middle-sized organizations in the

Aston sample that were most centralized, whereas the very large and very small were decentralized. This dynamic was not apparent in the data presented in this study, however, since only cross-sectional data were analysed statistically. The Aston data, which was focused on structural and functional elements of organizations, ought to provide a possible link to the elements of organizational culture revealed in the Ghiselli questionnaire, but the links are tenuous. It was thought that high levels of centralization, formalization and standardization might be expected to correspond to high administrative, managerial and problem-solving scores. However, this correspondence was only found with two companies in the sample — the Agency and the Stores Group — and the conclusion was drawn that the comparison was false, if only because there was a sufficiently high correlation between formalization and standardization to indicate that the two are probably different names for the same variable. One is forced to the conclusion, with Payne and Pugh (1976) that 'structure' is interdependent with organization culture and that structural analysis needs to be supplemented by measures of culture if we are to understand more fully variations in organizational functioning and performance. However, the Aston data was shown to fit moderately well within the Harrison framework, arranged as a four-cell matrix along the two dimensions of centralization and formalization, and this seems to indicate that Harrison's analysis is essentially 'structural' and makes less allowance for differences in behaviour within organizational cultures. Where technology (manufacturing) is a less directly important cultural determinant than the type of person employed, e.g. in service industry, the Ghiselli method reveals significant differences between organizations. To repeat, this demonstrates the sterility of trying to show that organizational culture is *determined* by structural factors.

Future research

Corporate culture has loosely been described in the popular academic press as the glue that holds organizations together —that is, something invisible that performs a stabilizing function, and a remedy to compensate for deficiencies in design or engineering. Like many such ideas, this is a consensus concept. We can all agree that organizations consist of groups that are different in some way from the general run of people, and we have been told by anthropologists that big groups of people, such as tribes, have cultures. Therefore, corporations must have cultures. Some authors go further and insist that the culture is reflected most accurately in the corporate mythology. But perhaps the concept itself is a myth created only to give a feeling of cohesion and a sense of purpose to workers beset by a fear of anomie. As Evan (1968) and Guion (1973) (both rigorous methodologists) have pointed out, culture is at best a 'commonsense idea', at worst a 'fuzzy concept'; if it is immeasurable it can only be a 'theology' created by the founder or a begetting idea (if there is no founder) incarnate in the temporal leader of the organization and his apostles. Such a mythology may be created by the company 'high priests', in order to secure conformity and perhaps to generate the guilt for failure so necessary to the Protestant work ethic. Maybe the academics are becoming interested in culture only now that the ethic itself is passing into history. If managerial work continues to be done, yet is deprived of benefit of meaning, then culture is no longer a necessary ingredient in the work situation and becomes an academic subject in every sense of the word. Then the proper tools for describing it are those of the theologian and not the social scientist. Yet it is apparent that leaders of organizations still regard it as a meaningful concept, creating and using it to achieve their ends, so we cannot altogether dismiss it as a public relations exercise, particularly if it is intuitively acceptable that people create their own worlds in which they figure prominently, if not in a starring role; and these worlds are fashioned out of the age in which they live and the values they have absorbed. If this is true, then the structures within which they work, the work that they do and the abilities and needs they have developed are all clues to the culture to which they subscribe as paid-up members of the 'club', even if not on the committee. So, if there is anything tangible to report, something at least should have stuck to the three coarse-meshed sieves (literature, histories and psychometrics) used in this book; and there should hopefully be enough common evidence to provide the basis for a theory of managerial culture. However, we cannot assume that the managerial culture pervades the whole workforce. One can only hope for a minimal degree of agreement between the leaders and the top management. Let us look then, again, at the evidence to see whether there are enough common threads to construct a web of theory sufficient to trap the truth. Furthermore, when constructing this web we must, as Hudson (1978) has said, endeavour to produce the best reading available, not merely one that fits the facts, however described.

We may perhaps begin with the people whose traits were analysed here since the calculations do actually show, first, that groups of people in one organization can be distinguished from people in another; and secondly that there are different types of people. An attempt to conceptualize these 'facts' leads to the inference that the organizations distinguish themselves along three variables — administration, management of people and problem-solving —and the people themselves fit into one of eight possible combinations of these three dimensions ('high' or 'low' in). The Aston data shows that manufacturing organizations tend to be 'high' in problem-solving — hence, one assumes, that group's preoccupation with the extent to which people control the workflow or the workflow controls the people ('line control of workflow'). However, the evidence concerning the provenance and relationships between centralization and formalization is less convincing, although there are some clear indications for the former, such as dependence upon external bodies such as holding companies, trade unions or suppliers. All we can infer is that *some* organizations must be perceived as more highly structured and centralized than others (otherwise they could not have been measured) and there may be an external reason for this.

However, it is important to remember that the Aston questionnaires were not filled in entirely by researchers, but also by organization members, so we are still handling perceptions. Indeed, were we to believe James and Jones (1974), psychological climate is the correct term for organizational culture. So administrative structure may be a part of the perceived culture and authors like Simon (1945), Porter and Lawler (1965), Pritchard and Karasick (1979), Ellis and Child (1973), Johnston (1976), Sutton and Rousseau (1979), and Kosticki and Mrela (1983) all believe that it is an important contribution to culture. Significantly, the most prolific of these researchers, Porter and Lawler, wrote that they wished they had included, in their study, an examination of variables such as 'personalities, values and communication patterns', and this remark prompts us to consider the three elements of personal culture discerned in Chapter Four as joint contributors rather than alternative solutions. Indeed, were we to adopt the psychoanalytic approach to the problem advocated by Kets de Vries and Miller (1984) we might advance the proposition that each dimension is but a different state of the group's psyche: 'dependence' representing the administrative state, 'pairing' the managerial state, and 'flight/flight' the problem-solving state.

It is apparent that many of the studies mentioned in Chapter Two have endeavoured to spread over the three areas, while generally taking as their point of entry the human reources problems — job satisfaction, performance, morale, leadership and the rest. Litwin and Stringer (1968) endeavoured to deal with the whole problem by laboratory simulation, but probably measured the wrong variables. They did not have much to say about culture as a product of the people concerned in the study (since the people were unacculturated students this might have been difficult anyway). Those who concerned themselves uniquely with people as providers of culture, such as Schneider and Bartlett (1968), Sofer (1961) or Ekvall (1983), usually came upon the concept of leadership as the dominant variable. But leaders accentuate different dimensions, so this leads away from leadership style *per se*. Only Mumford (1981) has attempted a systematic investigation of the ethical aspects of culture, as if it were the epitome of a grouping based upon professional expertise. Such a proposition, which many may see as a polite form of operant conditioning, is at least concerned primarily with codes of behaviour.

Mumford is also concerned with peformance, and so too are the anthropologists, like Pettigrew (1979), Schall (1983), Riley (1983) and Bate (1984), although only the last advances an easily workable framework of criteria or dimensions. It is curious that there are so few studies of the way organizations solve problems as an insight into their culture, particularly as the business game invented by Hesseling was a source of good insights into national culture in the writer's previous study. This is possibly where the management training programmes described in Chapter Three are of interest, for they provide evidence of different approaches to the same problem. In the Agency the mounting of the programme was primarily an administrative and political activity. The topics must appear relevant to the proposed participants, otherwise they will make excuses and not come. On the other hand, the teachers must be acceptable to the politicians (in 1984, for example, it was necessary to find an adequate number of female speakers). In the stores group the accent has been upon the teaching of managerial skills, as we have indicated: after the last programme the course director was severely criticized for poor management of the programme. In the manufacturing company the course material had to be orientated towards the resolution of a currently perceived management problem: the dehumanization of the organization by excessive systemization. In the insurance broker too, the content has been problem-based but the participants are perceived as forming part of a group that needs to learn the capacity to manage corporately.

Although it is possible to argue that the programme director might be blinded by his pre-conceived perceptions or seek to influence the way the company behaves, nevertheless this theory is robust enough to withstand attempts to modify it: the agency refused to accept a draft programme which would have satisfied officers' (but not members') requirements, whereas the stores group did not criticize the entire content of their programme (although one part was seen as incompetent), nor did they discontinue it: they simply demanded a change of programme director. The manufacturing company, on the other hand, *did* discontinue theirs for a while. It is therefore possible to state with some certainty that management training is at once a reflection of, and attempt to, perpetuate (or modify) the managerial role culture, and Harrison's matrix can be reinterpreted as a statement of three (and possibly four) dimensions of culture (if we accept 'atomistic' as a dimension). However, as we have seen from the Aston data, organizations not specifically different in culture can be placed in different parts of the matrix using only contextual variables and this indicates that the model is inadequate as a taxonomy.

However, the taxonomy we have suggested, embracing as it does three independent variables, is shaky on at least two counts: it derives mainly from analysis of personal traits of people rather than being contextually based; and it does not explain why organizations attract different groups of people. Many philosophers of organization, such as Astley and Ven de Ven (1983), Kilmann (1983), Tung (1978) and Johne (1983) pay great attention to the environment as an important determinant of culture. Dimensions such as turbulent/placid, favourable/unfavourable, active/passive are used to describe the area outside the organization boundary, with which it must cope in order to survive and prosper. However, with this as with so many other concepts treated here, the problem is one of measurement. It may be, as Das (1983) has argued, that we should not seek to measure everything quantitatively — and certainly some of the studies reported here (and a good many more not reported) are more interesting for their insights than their statistics — but that does not excuse us from considering how they might be better measured, if this can be achieved economically. The present study lacks a useful means of categorizing, not only the existing environment, but the environment as it has been since those studied entered the organization. Moreover, we should need to monitor the organization's perception of its environment since it is not enough to determine objective turbulence. The environment is seen subjectively by organization members and this provides the *raison d'être* for what we have called the external culture, the face the organization presents to the world in order to engender 'customer' confidence. It is intuitively noticeable that the more organizations strive to present a self-confident exterior the more turbulent the internal culture; conversely, the more an organization is confident of its mission the less it troubles to present a united face to the world (it is expanding so rapidly that growth, not culture, provides the corporate 'glue').

So far as measurement of the degree of administrative orientation is concerned, the Aston data presents the best method we have seen. It is more systematic (if less interesting) than the Woodward method of counting heads and at least validates some of the Northcote Parkinson rules of thumb. It might be a better instrument if it had been better suited to the measurement of service organizations and of bureaucracies which concentrate more upon conversion than output and so are perforce more administratively inclined; however, these are not insuperable methodological problems.

So far as the measurement of attitudes and values is concerned, many writers have expressed prejudice against self-report questionnaires, especially those that attempt to elicit one set of values or attitudes. A study by Cairnes (1981) showed quite conclusively that businessmen, at least, can hold more than one set of values at any one time. For instance, businessmen who agreed that it was wrong to give bribes also agreed that it was right to give bribes if there was no fear of discovery. Cairnes showed that there is a hierarchy of values, just as Maslow had demonstrated, half a century earlier, a hierarchy of needs. Similarly, the values that people espoused arose from their social background, including their work experience. The values and attitudes can perhaps only be induced from careful observation of behaviour, and that is what the anthropologists would have us believe. Nevertheless, we cannot ignore the importance of the leader as the symbol of the culture of the followers; he can only lead them where they want to go, or where they feel they can go (the dilemma of socialist political leaders). It is here that Hofstede's 'Hermes' study was helpful in providing dimensions whereby the led can measure the leader in quite objective ways (the concept of masculinity/femininity as applied to leadership seems to have been insufficiently explored). Leach (1954), Cohen (1975), Hage and Dewar (1973) and Kotter and Lawrence (1974) have all drawn attention to the interaction of the leader with his immediate elite group as being a creative force of culture, and even simple tools such as those utilized by Weinshall (1979) should provide interesting and quasi-objective data in this respect.

Finally, the question of problem-solving behaviour arises. It has already been argued that treatment of common problems might provide useful comparative data, and it is possible to imagine problems such as recruitment, investment (and their opposites, retirement and disinvestment) as sources of useful comparative data. Bate (1984) has opened up a useful vein of riches. But ultimately we have to rely upon the insights and values of the commentator. It seems as if, with all its faults, the laboratory exercise is most likely to be of use in this area as the case study is notoriously value-laden. Having discussed the environmental problems, we turn now to examine the other basic weakness of this research.

It is worthwhile to make an observation about the origins of the groups of organization people analysed here. The main point to note is that the groups analysed here are by no means random. The total sample consists of those members of middle and senior management who were deemed worthy, by the organization, of investment in training. Since much of training is remedial ('knocking off the chips', 'rounding out' are expressions often used by the sponsors) it may be assumed that the business of management training is the discovery of managerial or problem-solving capacity in people who, in our terminology, have hitherto been 'fixers'. Training is thus a selection and screening process and an integrated training programme provides a series of hurdles or hoops that must be successfully negotiated by aspirants to the elite managerial group. If this is so, one might ask why the screening process is necessary at all. Would it not be simpler to measure individual capacities and recruit direct to the level required? In modern, high technology companies where personal obsolescence is at a high rate, this is happening. Corporate culture approximates to the sum of the individual cultures of members. Jaques (1961) and others have argued that each person has a natural ceiling. Surely the learning curve does not have to be so long? The answer lies perhaps in the need of elite groups to reconcile their view of the environment with that of new entrants. Because the former are half a generation older than the latter they are perhaps more interested in finding people who will operate according to their own parameters than in changing those parameters to fit the real world (as perceived by those who have more lately been totally immersed in it) while at the same time gradually adapting their own parameters so as to still be able to cope with environmental problems. Since they hold the tiller, it is essential not to 'rock the boat'. Selection and promotion is thus a process of rapid deceleration of participants towards the cruising speed of the organization.

People, however, are continually joining the organization and impregnating it with their own cultural background (home, education, class, economic affluence, life experience). All this is not abandoned upon joining the firm, but helps to create a new culture for that cohort of entrants. So the cultures examined here are those established by the elites and are applicable, in the main, to them only. Although elites seek to extend the culture downwards, they have relatively few instruments beyond rituals, rites of passage, controls, structures, the conduct of meetings and investment policies. Thus, corporate culture, far from being the glue that holds unstable organizations together, is simply a large lens held up by high priests through which the worshippers may examine their gods, the stars: 'You shall see things thus.' If the worshippers turn their heads away and look at one another, they will be less able to see a coherent picture, although it will undoubtedly be more realistic.

Does this mean that culture is an illusion, not worth study? Probably not, for it is the one thing that distinguishes one firm from another, gives it coherence and self-confidence and rationalizes the lives of those who work for it. Culture satisfies the basic needs for affiliation and security in attempting to describe as unified a grouping that may seem to be random. It is life-enhancing to be different, and safe to be similar, and culture is the concept that provides the means of accomplishing this compromise. It may therefore be argued that a new research strategy is required, one which investigates the various elements and processes of organization culture.

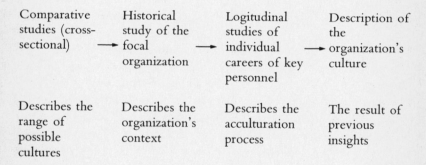

Figure 8.1 *A possible strategy for studying organizational culture*

Figure 8.1 describes one possible research strategy. First, a mechanical tool such as the Ghiselli SDI (or even a modified Aston instrument) is used to compare the focal organization with other organizations. At this stage the tool must show that there are significant differences, and establish a series of dimensions along which organizations can reliably be measured.

Having established that the focal organization is identifiably and objectively different from other organizations, a historical study should be undertaken in order to establish the context in which the focal organization exists. This has been shown to be an important element in the process, since it provides objective data concerning the important events in the organization's existence, as well as information about the industrial or commercial culture which the organization operates.

Once a good picture of the organization has been achieved it is important to understand the process by which the high priests of the culture reached their positions. In particular the selection processes (both initial and internal) should be studied, together with the key experiences that have influenced their careers, and the manner by which their values change from being general and community values to organization-dominated values. This information may be elicited partly from study of personnel records, and partly from semi-structured interviews with a representative sample of top management personnel.

With this data, it should be possible to make an accurate description of the culture of the organization, and hazard an educated guess as to whether the behaviour is appropriate to the context.

Clearly, this is only one of several possible strategies. The reason that it has been preferred by the writer is that, by beginning with a mechanical tool, questions are posed which it is the task of the other two methods to answer. The tool cannot be expected to provide a conclusive taxonomy of itself — the dimensions it generates are not of themselves sufficient explanation. Nor are the historical studies sufficient evidence of distinctions to be drawn because they are not easily comparable if the organizations are not from the same sector. Finally, although a study of the acculturation process to which senior personnel have been submitted may yield insights into the method by which the culture is transmitted, it cannot be expected to enable a description of the culture as a whole.

Figure 8.1 also seems to have significance at a more general level of abstraction. Much of the debate concerning cultural analysis has been over the definition, whether culture should include actual behaviour, or whether it should consist only of what is left when everything that is scientifically verifiable has been removed. There seems no reason to create a false dichotomy between belief and behaviour given that the two are bound to be interlinked. And the fact that empirical investigation is bound to be influenced by observer bias should not preclude all attempts in this direction. The stance of this book has been that there is a need for both specific studies (on the right of the figure) and general studies (on the left). Furthermore, the processual study of the flow of events in the life of the organization and its members forms the link between the two approaches, just as Chapter Three has served as a bridge between Chapters Two and Four.

Cultural analysis is, we believe, not only concerned with the analysis of individual needs for security and recognition, but also with the group as a group, and both approaches have been used by different schools of philosophy. What now seems certain is that cultural analysis must seek to draw on both schools of thought. In an interesting synthesis of the work of four cultural philosophers (Berger, Douglas, Foucault and Habermas), Wuthnow *et al.* (1984) conclude as follows:

> The uneasy stance that cultural theorists have taken towards positivism, therefore, does not rule out the possibility of pursuing cultural analysis as a rigorous empirical science. Because of its orientation toward the role of ideas in social life, cultural analysis is perhaps a somewhat more perceptive vantage point from which to recognise the biases inherent in scientific investigation itself. The analyst of culture is of necessity forced to acknowledge the interpretive impact of his or her own suppositions on the data and to recognise the value of these interpretations within particular cultural contexts despite their relativity. But this admission does not foreclose the possibility and desirability of seeking empirically verifiable generalisations about the patterning of cultural phenomena. [pp. 258-9.]

If, as we have suggested, both the perceived patterns of conformity-because-of-belief, conformity-despite-belief and nonconformity-because-of-belief in the cultural norms are all studied, as the central part of figure 8.1 seems to indicate, it should be possible to build taxonomies of managerial role culture more satisfying than the one suggested here.

A further research question, raised by Haire, Ghiselli and Porter over twenty years ago, remains unanswered: how far does corporate culture transcend national culture? This must depend upon the strength of the corporate culture. In companies like IBM and Shell culture is recognizable world-wide. Members of these companies often derive their social status from the organization they serve rather than from their culture of origin (i.e. 'who they work for, not what they do'). Similarly, as many experiments in this country have shown, it is possible to imprint the values and behaviour deriving from one culture onto the workforce of another with startling effect. Yet it is hard to see how this could happen without some kind of culture tolerance, even when allowance had been made for the sort of deviant behaviour demonstrated in the Milgram effect. Furthermore, as has been shown by the author in a previous cross-cultural study, cultures are not discrete — there is a considerable degree of overlap — so that apart from extreme cases of 'culture shock' where the culture of the organization is completely different from the national culture, it would seem possible that one or the other could dominate. In commercial organizations the shock might be likely to arise out of differing views about criteria for effective performance. It is a usual American strategy when acquisitions are made in foreign lands, to allow the new subsidiary to function almost autonomously, providing it continues to show a mutually acceptable return on capital. It is only where there are differences of view about this level that the parent company seeks to change the people, and the systems. In this sense we may conclude that the corporate beliefs, which must stem from national cultural beliefs about the nature of business, are dominant, and thus the national culture of the local subsidiary is moulded by the desires of the parent. But to effect these changes it is nearly always necessary (as Japanese and German companies have found in this country) to insert expatriate managers from the parent culture in the foreign subsidiaries and this leads to the conclusion that the culture of the organization is less strong than the culture of those who control it either directly or through the systems that they have designed. Where, however, there is a large degree of central control of financial performance then, sooner or later, the business culture of the multinational will prevail over both national and local corporate culture. Hence one might expect multinational corporations to employ in their subsidiaries a more administratively prone and problem-solving type of person, the 'consultant', and fewer autonomy-prone 'supervisors'. Thus the strength of an organization's culture depends upon the degree to which the various types of 'effective' manager in the organization, as defined by Ghiselli and modified by this study, are actually represented by manager orientations and managerial behaviour. For selection is the basic tool of culture-creation, and to understand culture, whether national or organizational, one must understand the process of selection by which it is created. This is why the Hofstede study does not, finally, quite ring true. He has, it would seem, measured variants of four dimensions of Hermes corporate culture, and this is perhaps why his variables do not sit well with the variables in this study. However, it would be foolish to suppose that this study is in any way definitive. Its purpose has only been to clarify the use of the word 'culture' in the organizational setting and to point the way to more effective comparative cultural studies.

Appendix: Some recent research

This appendix contains a review of the research carried out in the last fifteen years, since serious study of the subject began. The research may be classified as follows:

(1) Laboratory
(2) Field
(3) Historical or desk reviews
(4) Questionnaire surveys.

The research is not, as we shall see, distinguished by its quality so much as its quantity. As Payne *et al.* (1976) stated, the growth of empirical research has been achieved at the cost of conceptual development. They showed that there are three basic confusions in the literature:

(1) Organization climate tends to be limited to job satisfaction, despite the work of LaFollette and Sims (1975).
(2) Organization climate tends to be used sometimes to explain the behaviour of organizations, and sometimes that of individuals. See, for example, Kaczka and Kirk (1967).
(3) Most measurement tools seem to be affective rather than descriptive (e.g. 'I like to work here because . . .' see, in particular, Ekvall (1983)).

In their final analysis, they concluded that organizational climate can, or should, be described in terms of the aggregate understanding the organization as a whole (or a department or team) and should be descriptive. They only found one study that fits the bill — Pace's 1968 investigation into academic climates. This scarcity encapsulates the present-day problem.

Laboratory

In this category we put all research that takes place outside the firm in a special environment. We may sub-categorize into whether organization men were used in the research or not, and whether the device was cross-sectional, 'one-shot' or longitudinal. We may say of laboratory studies in general that they tend to over-simplify the problem by looking at one effect and observe it by using non-work-people (if one may so classify students). They do, however, admit of close and detailed study in a controlled environment and while the results themselves often border on the banal, the implications can sometimes be insightful, as in the Litwin study reported below. We shall report our own small laboratory study on subjectively perceived climate below.

Field

Field studies may also be sub-categorized into those that are cross-sectional and those that are longitudinal, and into one-firm and comparative studies. The problems with field studies are the wide variety of elements studied and the relative weakness of the tools used, but they do provide insights that are not available in the classroom — as, for example, the study by Greiner *et al.* of the Inland Revenue Service reported below. No amount of laboratory testing would have shown the existence of a back-up culture, a phenomenon we have shown to exist in our own research.

Desk reviews

These are by no means the least valuable of the research methods available, as Homans' (1950) seminal work proves. However, we are at the mercy of the writer's interpretation of what has been written, and we are looking at the data through two screens, thus increasing the opacity. On the other hand, because of the diverse nature of the data, we can hardly avoid published sources which help to make the life of the organization somewhat plainer.

Questionnaire surveys

These attempt to obtain subjective impressions of the concept climate and are often used to generate evaluation instruments. Because they are generalized findings from several firms, they tell us mainly about the subjectively felt impressions of the concept, which may reduce the variations to an irreducible minimum.

Laboratory longitudinal study on students

Litwin's (1968) study, which represents a refinement of the classic but blurred study by Lewin, Lippitt and White (1939), draws on the research of McClelland (1961) and the theory-building of Atkinson (1964). The model that Litwin set out to test runs as follows:

(1) All individuals have certain basic motives or needs. These motives represent behaviour potentials and influence behaviour only when aroused.
(2) Whether or not these motives are aroused depends upon the situation or environment perceived by the individual.
(3) Particular environmental properties serve to stimulate or arouse various motives.

Atkinson went on to try and apply subjective expected utility theory to these needs, but Litwin left this aside in his own experiment, which, like the Lewin, Lippitt and White experiment, set out to create three environments using the leader as the instrument.

Litwin obtained the results he predicted, namely that the achievement-orientated organization did best, the affiliation-orientated organization achieved the highest level of satisfaction and the power-orientated firm was the least innovative.

The interesting part of the study was revealed in a 'before-and-after' study using the California Psychological Inventory. Three scales indicated that significant changes had taken place: on self-acceptance, responsibility and commonality. The power-orientated organization members became less content with themselves, less accepting of others and more anxious and impatient, whereas the achievement-orientated organization members grew in responsibility, patience and resourcefulness, according to these scales. The importance of these scales lies in the idea that organizations can change personality traits. If this is indeed so, then personality traits are likely to reflect culture. Indeed, there is some possibility that the interaction of personality *creates* culture. If this is so, then we must look, not at the carpets and regulations, but at the aptitude tests and recruitment officers to understand culture.

Meadows (1980) has recently tried to show the effect of personality upon satisfaction with group structure. In this research he recognized two structures, organic and mechanistic, and he sorted his twenty-four small working groups according to his own instrument, so the possibility of research-bias is not to be discounted. Each of the groups contained three or four people ($n = 93$) so the unit of investigation is small and cannot help much with the main investigation. However, he did find that where individuals had strongly expressed needs (N. dominance, N. achievement, N. autonomy and N. deference), these people, although dissatisfied, suffered less frustration in organic groups than in mechanistic groups. Furthermore, people with strong traits were more frustrated than people with weak ones. Significantly, assertive managers (high on N. achievement, N. dominance and N. autonomy) were not correlated with high ingenuity; in other words, they were likely to be dissatisfied whether they found themselves in a mechanistic or organic working environment. This adds to the problem of finding the correct niche for the innovator/consultant.

However, there is little evidence that climate affects performance directly. Some people prefer one type of climate, some another. Thus, as McCarrey and Edwards (1973) pointed out, people will say the climate is propitious for performance if it suits their personality. Fulk and Wendler (1982) came to much the same conclusion.

Field studies

An interesting attempt to describe culture was made by Marshall (1982). She compared and contrasted two process production companies using four elements: the company's stock of managers (i.e. the profile); the job models managers use (analytical or holistic); the things that influence job performance (such as the technology and the market) and the managers' perceptions of freedom. The study is somewhat faulted in that the 'Ilex' company managers were technical specialists, whereas the 'Dais' managers had a predominantly sales bias, so inevitably their orientations were somewhat different. But it is an important linkage study in that it provides a person-based study of climate (i.e. climate as seen by participants via a framework); it enlarges the basic concept of Harrison's original model (she shows that two cultures can be demonstrated by induction rather than deduction); it reinforces the Stamp (1981) model of orders of learning (Dais managers operate on lower level (1 and 2) perceptual models and Ilex managers on somewhat higher (3 and 4)). Finally, the climatic conditions reinforce the perceptions that have been gained from this study. Marshall listed six major influences on organizational culture (and we shall show that these are indeed different for the organizations studied in this book). They are:

(1) Nature of the product and production technology.
(2) Organization structure, especially centralization or decentralization.
(3) Company's economic/market position.
(4) Company's recruitment policy.
(5) Officially promoted priorities.
(6) Organization's socialization mechanisms.

Hedlund (1978), in an examination of two highly similar companies with different cultures operating successfully in the same market, concluded that organizations can choose what culture to adopt — it is 'in the final analysis a matter of intrinsic rather than instrumental value' (p. 1). The 'Andante' company was informal and its effective operation rested upon human relationships: 'You have to have spent a long time in the company in order to be able to function . . .' (p. 6); 'you have to be brought up in the culture in order to function in it' (p. 7). He argued that the risk for this company was that 'an increasingly grave mismatch between environmental demands and organization inability to change might develop over time' (p. 70). He found it organized 'too loosely' (p. 8). 'Furioso', on the other hand, was much more mechanistic, and there was more control from the centre, with more specialization and standardization (p. 10), with less integration. There was more 'going into and out of the organization than in Andante' (p. 12). He noticed a stifling of initiative and a tendency to delegate upwards. In summary, 'nobody is irreplaceable in Furioso, whereas in Andante everybody is hard to replace' (p. 13). He attributed the differences in culture to:

(a) the president of the company
(b) the top managers who personify the culture
(c) style imprinting upon the individuals 'who assimilate it almost to the extent of making it part of their personalities'
(d) the self-reinforcing characteristics of the organization
(e) the organizational structure and process (which are 'determined by the culture and derive their meaning from it')
(f) its historical development.

Significantly, he rejected environmental influences: organization behaviour 'is not activity in the structured organization as a response to challenges in the environment but a process that can be viewed as taking place both in the abstract concept of the organization and the equally abstract concept of its environment' (p. 16) and he quoted Angyal (1941) and Meyer and Rowan (1977, p. 346) in support of his interactive model. He concludes that an affirmation of a break with past culture is proclaimed in the person of the new president of the corporation.

This analysis seems to mitigate the force of two possible influences on culture. First, it is not the environment that creates style, but the initial leadership. Environment can eventually, through causing performance failure, cause the organization to change its culture (or style, as Hedlund called it). Second, the leader may be partly the creator of the style and partly the product of it. The strongest force appears to be the nature and personality of the people employed, their career development patterns and the degree to which the imprinting process changes their personality.

An anthropological view of organization culture was taken by Pettigrew (1979). Using concepts such as beliefs, ideology, language, ritual and myth he attempted to chart the rise and decay of a boarding school. He discussed the place of the work of Donaldson (1972), Boswell (1972), Greiner (1972) and Strauss (1979) in analysing context structure and function of organization and placed heavy emphasis on the work of Selznick (1957) and Clark (1972) in describing organizations in terms of the creation of organizational character and sagas. His definition of organizational culture reflected his special interests: 'Culture is the system of such publicly and collectively accepted meanings operating for a given group at a given time. This system of terms, forms, categories and images interpret a people's own situation to themselves' (p. 574).

In other words, the object of culture is to give meaning to action, rather than defining it. Pettigrew recognized that this unitary concept 'lacks analytical bite' and proceeded to redefine culture as 'the source of a family of concepts. The offsprings of the concept of culture I have in mind are symbol, language, ideology, belief, ritual and myth. Of these, symbol is the most inclusive category' (ibid). He ended with a plea for the study of language as a clue to organization culture.

As an approach to the study of organization culture there can be no quarrel with Pettigrew's vision. The matter is only complicated when one attempts to operationalize it. Any comparative study must have recognizable parameters, and while it is tempting to fall into the trap of suggesting that each organization is unique, for comparative processes at any rate, this approach is not much good. Clearly the chief purpose of culture-building is to create commitment, and by studying the nature of commitment, such as Kanter (1972) and Buchanan (1974) have done, we shall come closer to understanding organizations, but, as Pettigrew points out, by citing McClelland, commitment is essentially a personal contract between the individual and the organization and may take a myriad of forms. In times of financial stringency commitment will be aroused through the pay packet; in times of expansion the trigger will be the chance to self-actualize.

In describing the organizations treated in this book, we have adopted an anthropological stance, if only to compare such an approach with the more statistical treatment afforded by the use of the Ghiselli instrument.

In an earlier paper, the importance of the entrepreneur in creating culture was stressed (Pettigrew (1977)). This concept is somewhat neglected in the article to which we have just referred, but may be useful in analysing organizations. As Pettigrew said, the interesting question is 'what does the entrepreneur make?' One of the answers to this question is 'myths'.

Leach (1954) and Cohen (1975) in studying myths have made two interesting propositions. The first is that a myth is a weapon deployed by individuals or groupings to justify stances and affirm power positions. The second is that myths explain and reconcile the contradiction between professed values and actual behaviour and legitimate established leadership systems faced with environmental threats. Pettigrew is led to conclude that the concept of myth has a powerful analytical role to play in studies of the creation of organizational cultures.

In an attempt to link myth-making with leadership, Wilkins (1984) tried to demonstrate that myths are important for the creation of culture: 'an important difference between excellent companies and the less successful companies is that the former have a clear set of concrete examples of past management actions . . . which make the philosophy come alive to participants' (p. 42). Although no workable system is provided, either in this article or in the somewhat more instrumental article on culture audit (1983), the useful distinction is made between human resource systems as symbols and as a context for culture: he suggests that they reflect and reinforce the cultural cues.

The anthropological approach suffers greatly from the problems of integration suggested by Das (1983). Schall (1983) endeavoured by a series of sorting processes to elicit communication rules that determined the climates in two groups in a large mid-western investment services corporation (the cultural significance of these words is not explained). Her general objective was basically to see how two interfacing work groups could develop different cultures, based upon identification of communication rules. She collected data by 'living in', by using questionnaires and by examining, interpreting and analysing documents. The results were disappointing, considering the effort involved. Where the 'rules' were different, they were not opposing; and they were often similar. There is hardly a difference between the following statements:

Group A: Avoid interpersonal confrontation.
Group B: Maintain a pleasant manner, no matter what [sic].
[p. 574.]

   Unfortunately she did not try to see how these climate statements relate to the general culture of the mid-western investment services corporation, and while it is clear that the author felt she had strongly differentiated, those seeking even a messy way of dealing with cultural taxonomy are not helped by this study.

   An even less methodologically respectable study was done by Bate (1984) along similar lines. This consisted of analysing the tape recordings and transcripts of interviews and meetings in three manufacturing companies. In this case there was no attempt to quantify the results. Consequently the findings are more interesting and the insights can at least be tested. Bate would like instruments to be constructed to measure the following cultural variables:

Unemotionality	(Affective orientation)
Depersonalization	(Allocation of responsibility to people of systems)
Subordination	(Hierarchical orientation)
Conservatism	(Change orientation)
Isolationism	(Do people like to work with others?)
Antipathy	(Rivalry between different groups e.g. management versus unions)

   He argued that all these elements were present to some extent in all organizations, but that the degree to which they varied was of critical interest in differentiating between cultures. Unfortunately the findings were not related to anything in the context of the companies studied, although he gave good examples of how the myth creates the reality of behaviour, as Wilkins had predicted.

Desk studies

Drexler (1977) using the Michigan technology and databank was able to produce convincing evidence that culture is organization specific and differs more between organizations than between units within organization. 'Climate has more variance attributable to organizations than to organizational sub-units, but consideration must be made to the fact that sub-unit differences do exist' (p. 40). Unfortunately, he made no attempt to classify the sorts of organization culture, nor did he go further than speculate about the influences upon culture, such as structure or environment.

While fully aware of the argument that the existing data is underutilized and that reanalysis of good, old data is preferable to the collection of poor, new data, it is important to bear in mind that the analysis can never exceed in accuracy the correctness of the initial data. and if there is a fault in the original data capture, this will not be recognized and eliminated during analysis. Attempts to reuse existing data tend to ignore that it is time-constrained (i.e. only applies for a limited time) and research constrained (i.e. was collected for particular purposes). For example, during the attempt to reanalyse the Aston data (see Chapter Five), errors of coding became apparent; these may not invalidate the original researchers' findings, but they do inhibit subsequent investigations.

Questionnaire studies

Litwin and Stringer (1968) reported an attempt to measure organizational climate using a six-scale instrument incorporating (pp. 67–8):

(1) Structure — the feeling the workers have about the constraints in their work situation; how many rules, regulations and procedures there are.
(2) Responsibility — the feeling of 'being your own boss', not having to double-check all your decisions.
(3) Risk — the sense of riskiness and challenge in the job and in the work situation.
(4) Reward — the feeling of being rewarded for a job well done; the emphasis on reward versus criticism and punishment.
(5) Warmth and support — the feeling of general good fellowship and helpfulness that prevails in the organization.
(6) Conflict — the feeling that management isn't afraid of different

opinions or conflict; the emphasis on settling differences here and now.

Questionnaires were administered to various groups, in particular to salesmen of electronic equipment ($n = 35$) and salesmen of computer time ($n = 19$). This study is of interest because it should show differences between the culture of a manufacturing firm and that of a service firm. The samples were small and only two significant differences were found: there was less structure but more warmth and support in the service firm. They also tested the motivations of the two groups, the service firm salesmen reporting significantly higher scores on need for achievement and (non-significant) lower scores for need for power (need for affiliation was about equal in both firms). They also asked the bosses of the salesmen to rate the salesmen's success on a four-point scale and correlated these results with the motivation scores of the individual salesmen separately for the two organizations. They found a significantly different correlation for need for achievement for the two firms: a positive correlation in the service firm and a negative one in the manufacturing firm. This may be related to the differences in the degree of felt structure and warmth and support. However, the study does not actually prove that there was more structure and warmth in one firm than in the other: this is the weakness of the study. The salesmen who were recruited to the two firms may have had these attitudes before they joined the firms and the findings, from the questionnaire, about the arousal effects of various culture aspects, while intuitively acceptable, are not conclusive. For the sake of future discussion we list them below, only the strongly supported hypotheses being given in Table A.1 (op. cit. pp. 90–1). The study from which this evidence is drawn was carried out on individuals and it will be seen that only pay is an arouser of achievement need.

In their earlier laboratory study they had endeavoured to demonstrate that need for achievement was aroused by creating a climate of informality, innovation, reward for excellent perfor-mance, support and warmth, cooperation and challenge and it is difficult to see why any other result should appear, since it was already known from the Lewin, Kippitt and White (1939) experiments that style of leadership is an important determinant of

Table A.1 *Litwin and Stringer's findings on strong arousal effects*

Perceived climate element	Need aroused		
	Achievement	Affiliation	Power
Structure		X	X
Responsibility		X	X
Warmth		X	
Support		X	
Reward	X	X	X
Conflict			X
Standards			
Identity		X	

productivity (although in that earlier experiment the autocratic style in fact produced greater productivity). It does not answer the question of perception — only that of reaction.

If their findings are to be believed, we need only look at the perceptions of managers in order to establish the culture. In particular, they stress

— perceived structure and constraint.
— warmth, support and encouragement.
— emphasis on reward versus punishment.
— perceived performance standards set by management.
— leadership style.

But why should not all these be dependent variables? How can we measure, through perceptions, a variable that is independent of them? By playing down (on p. 188) the importance of the history of the firm, the technology and the needs, values and initial expectations of the members they seem, like the anthropologists following Pettigrew, to negate the real-life importance of these aspects, and ignore their earlier finding that need for achievement is not a correlate of individual, but only organizational success. In other words, they ignore the creators of culture, the managers themselves.

Questionnaire surveys of businessmen

Tagiuri (1968) in an attempt to discover the primary dimensions of executive climate, developed a checklist of over two hundred statements about 'my business' which he asked 232 executives to rate from 0 to 7 to the degree that they described the respondent's own business. He then applied factor analysis to discover those factors which varied independently. He explained about 50 per cent of the variance using five factors of which 17.9 per cent was the quality of direction and guidance, 10.5 per cent was the quality of superiors, 9.7 per cent was the quality of the workgroup and just over 6 per cent each came from the professional atmosphere and emphasis upon results (with autonomy). These results are hardly surprising but they do indicate the importance of the sort of person joining the company to the climate, a finding hinted at by Pace (1968). Tagiuri himself concluded that (p. 240) 'specific organizations may have unique characteristics that override the importance of the variables highlighted by the classification proposed and that invalidate it as a good way of giving a reasonably 'good' description of that particular executive climate' [sic].

Meyer (1968) reported an attempt to devise an instrument for measuring climate in General Electric, using the following elements (pp. 155-6):

Amount of structure perceived
Feelings of responsibility
High standards set
Fair rewards given
Supportiveness of supervisors and associates
Amount of conflict tolerated
Degree of good fellowship
Degree of identity felt.

Meyer showed that the plant which had a below-average score on structure and higher than average score on all other items was 'unusually successful' in relation to its competitors, whereas a plant where the scores were the opposite was 'somewhat less successful' than its competitors. As a result of factor analysis, Meyer reduced the eight factors to six:

Constraining conformity
Responsibility

Standards
Reward
Organizational clarity
Friendly, team spirit.

Unfortunately, this study tells us nothing about the causes of the climate. The interesting item in the account is the fact that structure may be both a 'desirable' and 'undesirable' characteristic of organizations. In the second questionnaire, 'amount of structure perceived' gives way to 'constraining conformity' (undesirable) and 'organizational clarity' (desirable). We may therefore eliminate actual structure as a sole determinant of culture, since it is so ambiguous, while retaining the importance of perception of structure.

One of the very rare studies using Harrison's organizational culture ideas was carried out as part of a wider study of social service departments by Kakabadse (1982). He used his own interview questionnaire to elicit views on the following aspects of culture:

Challenge and responsibility
Conflict
Warmth and support
Performance.

It will be seen that the questions owe much to Child's concepts, and the Harrison questionnaire does not appear to have been administered. The results are somewhat confusing and the characteristics listed in his Table 3.7 do not accord with those expected of the cultural stereotypes. For this reason his otherwise interesting finding is open to question. His finding was that there are three cultures in Social Service departments: a power culture at the top — with departmental managers fighting each other for resources; a role culture in the centre, maintaining the homeostatic mechanisms; and a task culture at the grass roots, dealing with the case-work (p. 109). It is often stated that organizations have several cultures, not one, and therefore it is crucial that there should be gatekeepers who can integrate the different cultures. It does not, however, solve the problem of external culture (the image one presents to the outside world), whether of condescending efficiency (e.g. 'You want the best seats — we have them'), or chaotic but willing service (e.g. 'You don't have to be mad here but it helps'). However, the conflict may not be total. One senior interviewee stated 'I have learnt that we are local government officers first and a [sic] social worker second. So there are constraints to begin with that nobody can act outside the law and nobody can act outside their policy' (p. 114).

Perhaps an explanation of Kakabadse's findings might lie in the fact that at the social work level, the social workers are an anti-organization culture. On the other hand, at top levels the reference group is the elected membership — the culture is that of the council chamber. Otherwise, his theory contravenes the theory that the culture-givers are at the top of the organization. It is also probable that he has confused culture with climate and is rediscovering the Blau and Scott (1963) finding that organizations are sandwiches of organismic and mechanistic tiers. This makes sense of his diagram, so that an autocratic tier is supported by an autocratic and formalized tier, which in turn is supported by a formalized democratic tier.

Greiner, Leitch and Barnes (1968) reported an interesting longitudinal study of a government bureaucracy. While the overall culture was somewhat autocratic, they discovered different climates in different departments and different factors affecting different sets of relationships. More importantly, they discovered what they called a back-up climate which was related to but not the same as the dominant climate. In this case, the dominant climate was directing, whereas the back-up climate was integrating. The researchers were using the Blake–Mouton grid and it will be remembered that both styles contain a high degree of task orientation, but the back-up climate contains, additionally, concern for people (see Blake and Mouton (1964)). They continued:

> We suggest that back-up climates are generated over the years in organizations because adherence to a single dominant climate is likely to prove impossible for guiding the behaviour of all people in all situations. Moreover, we can speculate that the rank order of back-up climate may be determined by the degree of compatibility and reinforcement given by each back-up climate to the dominant climate. [pp. 207-9]

The importance of this study for our purposes is that the culture was perceived to be generated by the *task* rather than the *people* at the top of the organization.

> These various findings suggest rather clearly that a district's organizational climate was rooted in factors largely outside its control — policies and programs from the national headquarters and regional offices, prescribed task relationships and required job functions. These impersonal forces were apparently so strong that employee preferences and experiences made little difference in determining the actual climate. [p. 214]

This gives us a second determinant of culture — the technology. The researchers ultimately questioned the desirability of a dual culture calling it 'a heavy psychological and organizational burden'. However, a moment's thought enables us to see it is necessary. The relative attractions of some organizations must lie in the ambiguity of their culture: enabling different people to live together with mutual agreement upon the (ambiguous) culture.

In a typically humorous piece of research upon the match between climate expectations of people joining insurance agencies and the actual climate they find, Schneider (1975) found some weak correlations between expectations, discovery and performance, particularly with one agency enjoying a highly supportive and conflict-free climate, according to its workers. Despite his reservation that the correlations, being weak, made 'any attempt at explanation more than the usual gamble' (p. 464) the evidence points to the desirability of achieving a match between the new agent's expectations of climate and his perception of it if the new agent is to be successfully motivated. It is also interesting to note that, whereas a 'good' climate helps performance, a 'bad' climate may not necessarily hinder it. He concluded that it is an attribute of good organization to create realistic job expectations.

Sutton and Rousseau (1979) examined the relationship between individual managers and the structure, technology and environment of the firms they worked for. Their 155 managers came from fourteen organizations in the public and private sectors in California. The number of managers interviewed ranged from one to twenty-nine. They found that environmental and organizational characteristics were related to job perceptions such as autonomy and participation, and individual responses about such matters as propensity to leave, innovation, stress and pressure. They suggested that 'dependence on the parent organization for supplies and reliance on its control hamper innovation and may increase the stress and pressure that managers experience'. However, Fulk and Wendler (1982) found that satisfaction is related to supervisory techniques but not performance.

In a lengthy consideration of the meaning of values, Mumford (1981) tried to demonstrate that man uses his value system to make sense of the world in which he finds himself. She defined (on p. 16) values, following Kluckhohn in Parsons and Shils (1951) as follows:

A value is a conception, explicit or implicit, distinctive of an individual or characteristic of a group, of the desirable which influences the selection from available modes, means and ends of action . . . It should be emphasised here, however, that affective (desirable), cognitive (conception) and conative (selection) elements are all essential to this notion of value. This definition takes culture, group and the individual's relation to culture and place in his group as primary points of departure. [p. 395.]

She went on to quote Bateson to show that these values are culture-specific:

The individual is needlessly simplifying, organizing and generalizing his own view of his own environment; he constantly imposes on this environment his own constructions and meanings; these constructions and meanings are characteristic of one culture, as over against another. [Hunt (1944), p. 723.]

She cavilled at his word 'needlessly', citing theories of homeostasis and mental equilibrium (op. cit., p. 16). She then proceeded to construct questionnaires based on Talcott Parsons, for use in four different environments (two firms, a bank and the Civil Service Department). The questionnaires covered subjective responses in five areas (p. 37).

Compliance values — a belief in strict discipline
Conformity values — a belief in an emphasis on efficiency and high
production
Performance values — a belief in an emphasis on efficiency and high
production.
Task values — a belief in tightly structured tasks.

She gave this questionnaire, arranged along a continuum, to thirteen computer systems designers, eleven user-managers, six senior managers, and 436 clerks of various sorts, spread over four firms. Her overall finding shows little discrepancy between the four sub-samples, the clerks' perceptions tending more towards what she calls the 'X' end of the continuum and the eighteen managers (there is no discrepancy in the tables) more to the 'Y' end. Equally unsurprisingly, the clerks' preferred values are, if anything, slightly more 'Y' in tone, although the differences are only brought out by modal analysis.

By contrast with the managers, the clerks felt that there exists a multiplicity of different values and it is quite acceptable for employees to hold very different views on what the firm should be doing and how it should be doing it. On the other hand, they all agreed that the firm likes to have conformity in procedures and they disagreed with managers about norms for efficiency and structure. This is not a surprising finding and has been replicated in the classroom many times by the researcher using an instrument based upon the Maslow hierarchy of needs designed by Peter Smith at Ashridge Management College. It does, however, cast doubt upon the concept that organizations may have separate and different cultures: the only theory that would allow these findings and maintain the concept is one which states that occupational subcultures are stronger than total organizational cultures. For while we dare not build theories on findings from a handful of managers, we cannot disregard the similarities in the 'verdicts' of the clerks, whose views are unmistakably similar, namely that while organizations may or may not allow individuals freedom in the ethical and performance areas, they seek to effect compliance and conformity through structuring the task.

Accordingly, we must not disregard the nature of the task performed by the managers in our own sample, so far as these are not general. However, one is forced to the conclusion that simply giving questionnaires to clerks will not establish a clear view of organizational culture, and that some other methodology must be found.

Johne (1983) reported an interesting experiment to see whether structure (as measured by the Aston scales) varies according to strategy and mode of operation in sixteen firms in the instrument manufacturing industry. He distinguished between firms in the positional mode (introducing new products mainly in response to market pressure) and those in the innovative mode (who lead the market in introducing new products proactively). He found that the structural elements varied according to which stage the company was at in innovation. For innovative companies there was medium formalization and centralization in the initiating stage and high formalization and centralization in the implementation stage; with the positional companies there was high formalization and centralization at the initiating stage and this was only slightly attenuated at the implementation stage. He also attempted to relate his findings to the Harrison model and found that the innovative firms used the 'task' style and positional firms the other three! Unfortunately, there is no discussion of this categorization but it would seem from his evidence that it is more likely that positional (reactive) firms are role cultures and innovative firms are more likely to be power culture, the implementation stage being a spin-off from the main culture, as expressed in the strategy, since Woodward has demonstrated that the technological demands of the implementation stage would move both sets of firms into a role-type sub-culture. There is plenty of evidence of different sub-cultures within organizations. What has interested us in this investigation is the dominant culture.

Bibliography

Abegglen, J.C. (1958), *The Japanese Factory*, New York, Free Press.

Adams, J.S. (1963), 'Toward an Understanding of Inequity', *Journal of Abnormal and Social Psychology*, **57**, pp. 422–36.
57, pp. 422-36.

Albrook, R.C. (1967), 'Participation Management — Time for a Second Look', *Fortune*, May, p. 167.

Allen, R.F. and Pilnick, S. (1973), 'Confronting the Shadow Organization', *Organizational Dynamics*, Spring, pp. 3-18.

Andrews, J.D.W. (1967), 'The Achievement Motive and Advancement in Two Types of Organization', *Journal of Personality and Social Psychology*, **6**, pp. 163-8.

Angyal, A. (1941), *Foundation for a Science of Personality*, New York, The Commonwealth Fund/Oxford University Press.

Asch, S. (1946), 'Forming Impressions of Persons', *Journal of Abnormal and Social Psychology*, Vol. 60, pp. 288-90.

Astley, W.G. and Van de Ven, A.H. (1983), 'Central Perspectives and Debates in Organization Theory', *Administrative Science Quarterly*, **28**, pp. 245-73.

Atkinson, J.W. (1964), *An Introduction to Motivation*, Princeton, Van Nostrand.

Bacharach, S.B. and Lawler, E.E. (1980), *Power and Politics in Organisations: The Social Psychology of Conflict Coalitions and Bargaining*, San Francisco, Jossey-Bass.

Bagehot, W. (1915), *The English Constitution*, London, Longman.

Bakke, E.W. (1966), *Bonds of Organisation*, Hamden, Connecticut, Archon Books.

Bales, R.F. (1970), *Personality and Interpersonal Behaviour*, New York, Holt, Rhinehart & Winston.

Bate, S.P. (1984), 'The Impact of Organizational Culture on Approaches to Organizational Problem-solving', *Organization Studies*, **5**, No. 1, pp. 43-66.

Belbin, R.M. (1981), *Management Teams: Why They Succeed or Fail*, London, Heinemann.

Bennis, W. (1977), 'Leadership', *The McKinsey Quarterly*, Autumn, p. 45.

Berne, E. (1964), *Games People Play: the Psychology of Human Relationships*, London, Andre Deutsch.

Bion, W.R. (1961), *Experiences in Groups and Other Papers*, London, Tavistock Publications.

Blake, R.R. and Mouton, J.S. (1964), *The Managerial Grid: Key Orientations for Achieving Production Through People*, Houston, Texas, Gulf Publishing Co.

Blau, P.M. and Scott, W.R. (1963), *Formal Organizations*, London, Routledge & Kegan Paul.

Boswell, J. (1972), *The Rise and Decline of Small Firms*, London, Allen & Unwin.

Bowers, D.G. (1969), *Work Organizations as Dynamic Systems*, Technical Report, 30 September, Institute of Social Research, University of Michigan, Ann Arbor, Michigan.

Brewster, C.J., Gill, C.G. and Richbell, S. (1983), 'Industrial Relations Policy: A Framework for Analysis'. In Thurley, K.E. and Wood, S. (eds.), *Industrial Relations and Management Strategy*, Cambridge, Cambridge University Press.

Brousseau, K.R. (1978), 'Personality and Job Experience', *Organizational Behaviour and Human Performance*, **22**, pp. 235-52.

Bruner, J. (ed) (1966), *Studies in Cognitive Growth*, New York, Wiley.

Buchanan, B. (1974), 'Building Organizational Commitment: The Socialization of Managers in Work Organizations', *Administrative Science Quarterly*, **18**, pp. 533-46.

Burke, W.W. (1972), 'The Demise of O.D.', *Journal of Enterprise Management*, **1**, No. 3, pp. 57-63.

Burns, J.M. (1978), *Leadership*, New York, Harper & Row.

Burns, T. and Stalker, G.H. (1961), *The Management of Innovation*, London, Tavistock.

Cairnes, W.J. (1981), 'A Study of Managers' Views about Corporate Social Responsibility', Unpublished D.Phil. thesis, Oxford.

Campbell, J.P., Dunnette, M.D., Lawler, E.E. III and Weick, K.E. (1970), *Managerial Behavior, Performance and Effectiveness*, New York, McGraw-Hill.

Carlsson, B. et al (1978), 'Learning and Problem-solving', *Sloan Management Review*, Spring.

Chandler, A.D. (1966), *Strategy and Structure*, New York, Anchor Books.

Child, J. (1972), 'Organisational Structure Environment and Performance — The Role of Strategic Choice', *Sociology*, **1**, p. 4.

Child, J. (1973), 'Strategies of Control and Organisational Behaviour', *Administrative Science Quarterly*, **18**, pp. 1-17.

Chinoy, E. (1952), 'The Tradition of Opportunity and the Aspirations of Automobile Workers', *American Journal of Sociology*, pp. 58, 453-9.

Clark, B.R. (1972), 'The Organisational Saga in Higher Education', *Administrative Science Quarterly*, **17**, pp. 178-84.

Cohen, A.P. (1975), *The Management of Myths: The Politics of Legitimation in a Newfoundland Community*, Manchester University Prss.

Cotgrove, S. in Griffiths, R.F. (ed) (1981), *Dealing With Risk*, Manchester University Press, pp. 122-40.

Crozier, M. (1965), *Le Monde des Employés de Bureau*, Paris, Editions de Seuil.

Cyert, R.M. and March, J.G. (1963), *A Behavioral Theory of the Firm*, Englewood Cliffs, New Jersey, Prentice–Hall.

Das, T.H. (1983), 'Qualitative Research in Organisational Behaviour', *Journal of Management Studies*, **20**, No. 3, pp. 301-11.

Deal, T.E. and Kennedy, A.A. (1982), *Corporate Cultures: The Rites and Rituals of Corporate Life*, California, Addison-Wesley.

de Board, R. (1978), *The Psychoanalysis of Organizations*, London, Tavistock.

Dieterly, D.L. and Schneider, B. (1974), 'The Effect of Organisational Environment on Perceived Power and Climate: A Laboratory Study', *Organisational Behaviour and Human Performance*, **11**, pp. 316-37.

Dill, W.R. (1978), *Running the American Corporation*, Englewood Cliffs, New Jersey, Prentice-Hall.

Dixon, N. (1976), *On the Psychology of Military Incompetence*, London, Jonathan Cape.

Donaldson, L. (1972), 'Forecasting the Future Trend of Bureaucratization', London Graduate School of Business (mimeo).

Drexler, J.A. (1977), 'Organisational Climate: Its Homogeneity Within Organisations', *Journal of Applied Psychology*, **62**, No. 1, pp. 38-42.

Dumont, L. (1970), *Homo Hierarchicus*, London, Weidenfeld & Nicholson.

Dunnette, M.D. and Campbell, J.P. (1970), 'Laboratory Education: Impact on People and Organisations'. In Dalton, G.W. and Lawrence, P.R. (eds), *Organizational Change and Development*, Homewood, Ill., Richard D. Irwin Inc./ The Dorsey Press.

Durkheim, E. (1933), *The Division of Labor in Society*, New York, Free Press.

Ekvall, G. (1983), *Climate, Structure and Innovativeness of Organisations*, Stockholm, Swedish Council for Management and Organisation Behaviour.

Ekvall, G. and Arvonen, J. (1984), *Leadership Styles and Organisational Climate for Creativity: Some Findings in One Company*, Stockholm, Swedish Council for Management.

Eldridge, J.E.T. and Crombie, A.D. (1974), *A Sociology of Organizations*, London, George Allen & Unwin.

Ellis, T. and Child, J. (1973), 'Placing Stereotypes of the Manager into Perspective', *Journal of Management Studies*, **10**, No. 4, pp. 234-55.

Emery, F.E. and Trist, E.L. (1965), 'The Causal Texture of Organisational Environments', *Human Relations*, **18**, pp. 21-32.

Evan, W.M. (1968), 'A Systems Model of Organizational Climate'. In Tagiuri, R. and Litwin, G.H. (eds), *Organizational Climate: Explorations of a Concept*, Boston, Harvard University.

Field, R.H.G. and Abelson, M.A. (1982), 'Climate: A Reconceptualisation and a Proposed Model', *Human Relations*, **35**, No. 3, pp. 181-201.

Fineman, S. (1975), 'The Work Preference Questionnaire: A Measure of Managerial Need for Achievement', *Journal of Occupational Psychology*, **48**, pp. 11-32.

Forehand, G.A. and Van Haller Gilmer, B. (1964), 'Environmental Variation in Studies of Organisation Behaviour', *Psychological Bulletin*, **62**, No. 6, pp. 361-82.

Franklin, J. (1975), 'Relations Among Four Social Psychological Aspects of Organisations', *Administrative Science Quarterly*, **20**, September, pp. 422-33.

French, W.L. and Bell, C.H. (1973), *Organization Development: Behavioral Science Interventions for Organization Improvement*, Englewood Cliffs, New Jersey, Prentice Hall.

Fulk, J. and Wendler, E.R. (1982), 'Dimensionality of Leader–Subordinate Interactions: a Path–Goal Investigation', *Organizational Behaviour and Human Performance*, **30**, pp. 241-64.

Gerwin, D. (1979), 'Relationships Between Structure and Technology at the Organisational and Job Level', *Journal of Management Studies*, **16**, No. 1, pp. 70-9.

Ghiselli, E.E. (1963), 'Intelligence and Managerial Success', *Psychological Reports*, **12**, 898.

Ghiselli, E.E. (1971), *Explorations in Managerial Talent*, Pacific Palisades, California, Goodyear Publishing Company, Inc.

Giddens, A. (1979), *Central Problems in Social Thgeory*, Berkeley, California, University of California Press.

Gill, R.W.T. (1982), 'A Trainability Concept for Management Potential and an Empirical Study of its Relationship with Intelligence for Two Managerial Skills', *Journal of Occupational Psychology*, **55**, pp. 139-47.

Gouldner, A.W. (1954), *Patterns of Industrial Democracy*, New York, Free Press.

Gouldner, A.W. (1957), 'Cosmopolitans and Locals', *Administrative Science Quarterly*, **2**, pp. 281-306.

Graves, D. (ed) (1969), *Decision-making: A New Approach*, British Institute of Management (Luton Branch).

Graves, D. (1970), 'A Comparison of Management Role Behaviour in Three Factories of an International Electronics Company', M.Phil. dissertation, London University.

Graves, D. (1972), 'Reported Communication Ratios and Informal Studies in Managerial Work Groups', *Human Relations*, **25**, No. 2, pp. 159-70.

Graves, D. and Pandit, S. (1974), 'Consequences of a Change in Organisational Goals of an Organisation in the Port Industry', *Journal of Indian Society for Training and Development*, **4**, No. 4, July–August 1984, pp. 2-12.

Graves, D. (1976), *Organizational Change in a Port Operating Authority*, London, National Ports Council.

Graves, D. (1981), 'Individual Reactions to a Merger of Two Small Firms of Brokers in the Re-insurance Industry: A Total Population Survey', *Journal of Management Studies*, **18**, No. 1, pp. 89-113.

Gregory, K.L. (1983), 'Native-View Paradigms: Multiple Cultures and Culture Conflicts in Organisations', *Administrative Science Quarterly*, **28**, pp. 359-76.

Greiner, L.E. (1972), 'Evolution and Revolution as Organizations Grow', *Harvard Business Review*, **50**, pp. 37-46.

Greiner, L.E., Leitch, D.P. and Barnes, L.B. (1968), 'The Simple Complexity of Organizational Climate in a Governmental Agency', in Tagiuri, R. and Litwin, G.H. (eds), *Organizational Climate*, Boston, Mass., Harvard University.

Guion, R.M. (1965), *Personnel Testing*, New York, McGraw Hill Inc.

Guion, R.M. (1973), 'A Note on Organizational Climate', *Organizational Behaviour and Human Performance*, **9**, pp. 120-5.

Hage, J. and Dewar, R. (1973), 'Elite Values Versus Organizational Structure in Predicting Innovation', *Administrative Science Quarterly*, **18**, September, pp. 279-90.

Haire, M., Ghiselli, E.E. and Porter, L.W. (1963), 'Cultural Patterns in the Role of the Manager', *Industrial Relations*, **2**, pp. 95-117.

Haire, M., Ghiselli, E.E. and Porter, L.W. (1966), *Managerial Thinking: An International Study*, New York, John Wiley & Sons, Inc.

Handy, C. (1978), *Gods of Management*, London, Pan Books.

Harrison, R. (1972), 'Understanding Your Organization's Character', *Harvard Business Review*, May–June, pp. 119-28.

Hayward, G. and Everett, C. (1983), 'Adaptors and Innovators: Data from the Kirton Adaptor–Innovator Inventory in a Local Authority Setting', *Journal of Occupational Psychology*, **56**, pp. 339-42.

Hearn, H.L. and Stoll, P. (1975), 'Continuance Commitment in Low-Status Occupations: The Cocktail Waitress', *Sociological Quarterly*, **16**, pp. 105-14.

Hedberg, B.L.T. et al (1976), 'Camping on See-saws', *Administrative Science Quarterly*, **21**, pp. 41-64.

Hedlund, G. (1978), *Organisation as a Matter of Style*, EIASM Paper 78-15, April, pp. 1-23.

Heller, R.A. (1982), *The Business of Success*, London, Sidgwick & Jackson.

Hellriegel, D. and Slocum, J. (1974), 'Organizational Climate: Measures, Research and Contingencies', *Academy of Management Journal*, **17**, No. 2, June, pp. 255-80.

Henry, W.E. (1948), *Executive Personality and Job Success*, American Management Association, Personnel Series, No. 120.

Hesseling, P.T.M. (1982), *Effective Organization Research for Development*, Oxford, Pergamon Press.

Heydebrand, W.F. (1973), *Comparative Organizations: The Results of Empirical Research*, Englewood Cliffs, New Jersey, Prentice Hall.

Hofstede, G. (1980), *Culture's Consequences*, Beverley Hills, CA., Sage Publications.

Holdaway, E.A. et al (1975), 'Dimensions of Organisation in Complex Societies: the Educational Sector', *Administrative Science Quarterly*, **20**, pp. 37-57.

Holt, E.B. (1931), *Animal Drive and the Learning Process: an Essay Towards Radical Empiricism*, London, Williams & Norgate.

Homans, G.C. (1950), *The Human Group*, New York, Harcourt Brace Jovanovich.

Homans, G.C. (1961), *Social Behaviour: its Elementary Forms*, New York, Harcourt Brace Jovanovich.

Honey, P. and Mumford, A. (1982), *The Manual of Learning Styles*, Published by Peter Honey, Maidenhead.

Howe, J.G. (1971), 'Group Climate: an Exploratory Analysis of Construct Validity', *Organisational Behaviour and Human Performance*, **19**, pp. 106-25.

Hudson, L. (1978), *Human Beings*, St. Albans, Paladin Books.

Hunt, J.W. (1981), 'Applying American Behavioural Science: Some Cross-Cultural Problems', *Organisational Dynamics*, Summer, pp. 55-62.

Hunt, J. (ed) (1944), *Personality and Behaviour Disorders*, New York, Ronald Press.

Inkeles, A. and Levinson, D.J. (1968), 'National Character: the Study of Modal

Personality and Sociocultural Systems'. In Lindzey, G. and Aronson, E. (eds), Reading, PA., Addison–Wesley Publishing.

Inkson, J.H.K. et al (1968), 'Administrative Reduction of Variance in Organization and Behaviour'. Unpublished paper given to the British Psychological Society, Annual conference, April.

James, L.R. and Jones, A.P. (1974), 'Organisational Climate: A Review of Theory and Research', *Psychological Bulletin*, **81**, pp. 1096-112.

Jaques, E. (1951), *The Changing Culture of a Factory*, Tavistock, London.

Jaques, E. (1961), *Equitable Payment*, New York, Wiley.

Johannesson, R.E. (1973), 'Job Satisfaction and Perceptually Measured Organisation Climate: Redundancy and Confusion'. In Fry, M.W. (ed), *New Developments in Management and Organisation Theory*, (Proceedings of the 8th Annual Conference, Eastern Academy of Management, pp. 27-37.)

Johne, F.A. (1983), *The Organisation of Product Innovation in High Technology Manufacturing Firms*, City University Business School Working Paper No. 50, pp. 1-21.

Johnson, R.T. and Ouchi, W.G. (1974), 'Made in America (Under Japanese Management)', *Harvard Business Review*, **52**, No. 5, pp. 61-9.

Johnston, H.R. (1976), 'A New Conceptualisation of the Source of Organisational Climate', *Administrative Science Quarterly*, **21**, pp. 95-103.

Jones, A.P. and James, L.R. (1979), 'Psychological Climate: Dimensions and Relationships of Individual and Aggregated Work Environment Perceptions', *Organisational Behaviour and Human Performance*, **23**, pp. 201-50.

Jung, C.G. (ed) (1964), *Man and His Symbols*, London, Jupiter Books.

Kaczka, E.E. and Kirk, R.V. (1967), 'Managerial Climate, Work Groups and Organisational Performance', *Administrative Science Quarterly*, September, **12**, No. 2, pp. 253-72.

Kahn, R.L. et al (1964), *Organizational Stress: Studies in Role Conflict and Ambiguity*, New York, Wiley.

Kakabadse, A. (1982), *Culture of the Social Services*, Aldershot, Gower Press.

Kanter, R.M. (1972), *Commitment and Community*, Cambridge, Mass., Harvard University Press.

Kaplan, A. (1964), *The Conduct of an Inquiry*, San Francisco, Chandler.

Kasarda, J.D. and Janowitz, M. (1974), 'Community Attachment in Mass Society', *American Sociological Review*, **39**, pp. 328-9.

Katz, D. and Kahn, R.L. (1966), *The Social Psychology of Organizations*, New York, Wiley.

Kets de Vries, M.F.R. and Miller, D. (1984), 'Group Fantasies and Organisational Functioning', *Human Relations*, **37**, No. 2, pp. 111-34.

Kiesler, C.A. (1971), *The Psychology of Commitment: Experiments Linking Behaviour to Belief*, New York, Academic Press.

Kilmann, R.H. (1983), 'A Typology of Organisation Typologies', *Human Relations*, **36**, No. 6, pp. 523-48.

Kirton, M. (1980), 'Adaptors and Innovators in Organisation', *Human Relations*, **33**, No. 4, pp. 213-24.

Klein, M. (1959), Our Adult World and Its Roots in Infancy, *Human Relations*, **12**, pp. 291–303.

Kleiner, B.H. (1983), 'The Interrelationships of Jungian Modes of Mental Functioning with Organisational Factors', *Human Relations*, **36**, No. 11, pp. 997–1012.

Kluckhohn, C. (1951), 'The Study of Culture'. In Lerner, D. and Laswell, R. (eds), *The Policy Sciences*, Stanford, C.A., Stanford University Press.

Kolb, D.A. (1976), 'Management and The Learning Process', *California Management Review*, **XVIII**, No. 3, pp. 21-31.

Kostecki, M.J. and Mrela, K. (1983), 'The Incompatibility of Comparisons', *Organisation Studies*, **4**, No. 1, pp. 73-88.

Kotter, J.P. (1982), 'General Managers are not Generalists', *Organizational Dynamics*, Spring, pp. 5-19.

Kotter, J.P. and Lawrence, P.R. (1974), *Mayors in Action*, New York, John Wiley & Sons.

Kramer, M. (1974), *Reality Shock: Why Nurses are Leaving Nursing*, St. Louis, C.V. Mosby.

Kraut, A.I. (1969), 'Intellectual Ability and Promotional Success Among High-level Managers', *Personnel Psychology*, **22**, pp. 281-90.

Krech, D., Crutchfield, R.S. and Mallachey, E.L. (1962), *Individual in Society*, New York, McGraw Hill.

Lafollette, W.R. and Sims, H.P. (1975), 'Is Satisfaction Redundant with Organizational Climate?', *Organizational Behaviour and Human Performance*, **13**, pp. 257-78.

Lawler, E.E.III, Hall, D.T. and Oldham, G.R. (1974), 'Organizational Climate: Relationship to Organizational Structure, Process and Performance', *Organizational Behaviour and Human Performance*, **11**, pp. 139-55.

Leach, E.R. (1954), *Political Systems of Highland Burma*, London, Bell.

Lewin, K. (1951), *Field Theory in Social Science*, New York, Harper & Row.

Lewin, K., Lippitt, R. and White, R.K. (1939), 'Patterns of Aggressive Behaviour in Experimentally Created "Social Climates" ', *Journal of Social Psychology*, **10**, pp. 271-99.

Lewis, R. and Margerison, C. (1979), 'Working & Learning — Identifying Your Preferred Ways of Doing Things', *Personnel Review*, **8**, No. 2, pp. 25-9.

Lipset, S.M., Trow, M. and Coleman, J. (1956), *Union Democracy*, New York, Free Press.

Litwin, G.H. (1968), 'Climate and Motivation: An Experimental Study'. In Tagiuri, R. and Litwin, G.H. (eds), *Organizational Climate*, Boston, Harvard University Press.

Litwin, G.H. and Stringer, R.A. (1968), *Motivation and Organizational Climate*, Boston, Harvard University Press.

Lorenz, K. (1967), *On Aggression*, London, Methuen.

McCarrey, M. and Edwards, S. (1973), 'Organisational Climate Conditions for Effective Research Scientist Role Performance', *Organisation Behaviour and Human Performance*, **9**, pp. 439-59.

McClelland, D.C. (1961), *The Achieving Society*, Princeton, Van Nostrand.

McFeely, W. (1971), 'Multilayered Management', *The Conference Board Record*, 8, No. 3.

McGregor, D. (1960), *The Human Side of Enterprise*, New York, McGraw Hill.

Mabe, P.A. and West, S.G. (1982), 'Validity of Self-evaluation of Ability: a Review and Meta-analysis', *Journal of Applied Psychology*, 67, No. 3, pp. 280-96.

Madariaga, S. de (1928), *Englishmen, Frenchmen, Spaniards,* London, Oxford University Press.

Maisonrouge, J. (1983), 'The Education of a Modern International Manager', *Journal of International Business Studies*, Spring/Summer, pp. 141-4.

March, J.G. and Simon, H.A. (1958), *Organizations*, New York, Wiley.

Marenco, C. (1968), 'The Evolution of Conceptions About the Human Functioning of Organizations' (Unpublished paper).

Margulies, N. and Raia, A.P. (1978), *Conceptual Foundations of Organizational Development*, New York, McGraw Hill.

Marples, D.L. (1967), 'Studies of Managers — A Fresh Start?', *Journal of Management Studies*, 10, No. 3, pp. 282-99.

Marshall, J. and Stewart, R. (1981), 'Managers' Job Perceptions. Part I: Their Overall Frameworks and Working Strategies', *Journal of Management Studies*, 18, No. 2, pp. 177-89.

Marshall, J. (1982), 'Organizational Culture', *Group and Organization Studies*, 7, No. 3, September, pp. 367-84.

Meadows, U.S.G. (1980), 'Organic Studies, Satisfaction and Personality, *Human Relations*, 33, No. 6, pp. 383-92.

Menzies, I.E.P. (1970), 'The Functioning of Social Systems as a Defence Against Anxiety', Centre for Applied Social Research, London (mimeo).

Merton, R.J. (1957), *Social Theory and Social Structure*, New York, Free Press.

Meyer, H.H. (1968), 'Achievement Motivation and Industrial Climate. In Tagiuri, R. and Litwin, G.H. (eds), *Organizational Climate*, Boston, Harvard University.

Meyer, J.W. and Rowan, B. (1977), 'Institutionalized Organizations: Formal Structures as Myth and Learning', *American Journal of Sociology*, 83, No. 2.

Milgram, S. (1974), *Obedience to Authority*, Tavistock, London.

Millar, J. (1979), *British Management versus German Management*, London, Saxon House.

Mintzberg, H. (1975), 'The Manager's Job: Folklore and Fact', Harvard Business Review, July–August, pp. 49-61.

Mintzberg, H. (1983), *Structure in Fives*, New Jersey, Prentice Hall.

Mirels, H. and Garrett, J. (1971), 'The Protestant Ethic as a Personality Variable', *Journal of Consulting and Clinical Psychology*, 36, pp. 40-4.

Muller, H. (1970), *The Search for the Qualities Essential to Advancement in a Large Industrial Group*, The Hague, Shell.

Mumford, E. (1981), *Values Technology and Work*, The Hague, Martinus Nijhoff.

Myers, I.B. (1962), *The Myers-Briggs Type Indicator*, Princeton, New Jersey, Educational Testing Service.

Newman, W.H. (1953), Article in *Journal of Business*, 26, No. 4, pp. 211-23, reprinted as 'Basic Objectives which Shape the Character of a Company' in Wolf, W.D. (ed) (1964), *Management*, Belmont, CA., Wadsworth Publishing Company.

Nicholas, I. (1982), 'Organizational Climate and Strategic Decision-making', *Journal of General Management*, **7**, No. 3, Spring, pp. 57-71.

Nightingale, D.V. and Toulouse, J.-M. (1977), 'Toward a Multi-level Congruence Theory of Organization', *Administrative Science Quarterly*, **22**, June, pp. 264-80.

Ohmann, O.A. (1958), 'The Leader and the Led', *Personnel*, **35**, No. 3, pp. 8-15.

Ouchi, W.G. and Jaeger, A.M. (1978), 'Social Structure and Organisational Type'. In Meyer, M.W. et al (eds), *Environment and Organisations*, San Francisco, Jossey Bass.

Pace, C.R. (1968), 'The Measurement of College Environments'. In Tagiuri, R. and Litwin, G.H. (eds), *Organizational Climate*, Boston, Harvard University Press.

Parsons, T. and Shils, E. (1951), *Toward a General Theory of Action*, Boston, Harvard University Press.

Payne, R.L. and Mansfield, R. (1973), 'Relationships of Perceptions of Organisational Climate to Organisation Structure, Context and Hierarchical Position', *Administrative Science Quarterly*, **18**, pp. 515-26.

Payne, R.L., Fineman, S. and Wall, T.D. (1976), 'Organisational Climate and Job Satisfaction: A Coceptual Synthesis', *Organisational Behaviour and Human Performance*, **16**, pp. 45-62.

Payne, R.L. and Pheysey, D.C. (1971), 'G.G. Stern's Organisational Climate Index: A Reconceptualisation and Application to Business Organisation', *Organisational Behaviour and Human Performance*, **6**, pp. 77-98.

Payne, R.L. and Pugh, D.S. (1976), 'Organisation Structure and Climate'. In Dunnette, M. (ed), *Handbook of Industrial and Organisational Psychology*, Chicago, Rand McNally, pp. 1125-73.

Perrow, C. (1972), *Complex Organizations: A Critical Essay*, Chicago, Rand Mcnally.

Peters, T.J. (1980), 'Leadership: Sad Facts and Silver Linings', *McKinsey Quarterly*, Spring. Reprinted from the Nov/Dec Harvard Business Review.

Pettigrew, A.M. (1973), *The Politics of Organizational Decision-making*, London, Tavistock.

Pettigrew, A.M. (1977), *The Creation of Organisational Cultures*, European Institute for Advanced Studies in Management, Working Paper 11, pp. 1-38.

Pettigrew, A.M. (1979), 'On Studying Organisational Cultures', *Administrative Science Quarterly*, **24**, December, pp. 570-81.

Porter, L.W. (1962), 'Job Attitudes in Management', *Journal of Applied Psychology*, **45**; pp. 375-84, *and* **47**, pp. 141-8.

Porter, L.W. and Lawler, E.E.III (1965), 'Properties of Organisation Structure in Relation to Job Attitudes and Job Behaviour', *Psychological Bulletin*, **64**, pp. 135-48.

Porter, L.W., Lawler, E.E. III and Hackman, J.R. (1975), *Behavior in Organization*, New York, McGraw Hill.

Pritchard, R.D. and Karasick, B.W. (1973), 'The Effects of Organisational Climate on Managerial Job Performance and Job Satisfaction', *Organisational Behaviour and Human Performance*, **9**, pp. 126-46.

Pugh, D.S. and Pheysey, D. (1968), 'Some Developments in the Study of Organisations', *Management International Review*, **8**, pp. 97-107.

Pugh, D.S., Hickson, D.J., Hinings, C.R. and Turner, C. (1969), 'The Context of Organisational Structures', *Administrative Science Quarterly*, **14**, No. 1, pp. 91-114.

Quinn, R.E. and Cameron, K. (1983), 'Organisational Life Cycles and Shifting Criteria of Effectiveness: Some Preliminary Evidence', *Management Science*, **29**, No. 1, pp. 33-51.

Quinn, R.E. and Rohrbaugh, J. (1983), 'A Spatial Model of Effectiveness Criteria: Towards a Competing Values Approach to Organisational Analysis', *Management Science*, **29**, No. 3, pp. 363-77.

Reitz, H. and Jewell, L.N. (1979), 'Sex, Locus of Control and Job Involvement', *Academy of Management Journal*, **22**, pp. 72-80.

Riley, P. (1983), 'A Structurationist Account of Political Culture', *Administrative Science Quarterly*, **28**, pp. 414-37.

Rose, M. (1975), *Industrial Behaviour: Theoretical Development Since Taylor*, Harmondsworth, Penguin Books.

Rosenberg, M.J. (1960), 'Cognitive Reorganisation in Response to Hypnotic Reversal of Attitudinal Effect', *Journal of Personality*, **28**, pp. 39-63.

Sayles, L.R. (1963), *Behaviour of Industrial Work Groups*, New York, John Wiley & Sons.

Schall, M.S. (1983), 'A Communication–Rules Approach to Organizational Culture', *Administrative Science Quarterly*, **28**, pp. 557-81.

Schein, E. (1978), *Career Dynamics: Matching and Individual and Organizational Needs*, Reading, Mass., Addison Wesley Inc.

Schein, E. (1983), 'The Role of the Founder in Creating Organizational Culture', *Organizational Dynamics*, Summer, pp. 13-28.

Schein, E. (1984), 'Corporate Culture — Constraint or Opportunity for Strategy?', *Issues*, **1**, No. 1, pp. 4-10.

Schneider, B. (1975), 'Organizational Climates: an Essay', *Personnel Psychology*, **28**, pp. 447-79.

Schneider, B. (1975), 'Organizational Climate: Individual Preferences and Organizational Realities Revisited', *Journal of Applied Psychology*, **60**, No. 4, pp. 459-65.

Schneider, B. and Bartlett, C.J. (1968), 'Individual Differences and Organizational Climate. I: The Research Plan and Questionnaire Development', *Personnel Psychology*, **21**, pp. 323-33.

Schneider, B. and Reichers, A.E. (1983), 'On the Etiology of Climate', *Personnel Psychology*, **36**, pp. 19-39.

Scholl, R.W. (1981), 'Differentiating Organizational Commitment from

Expectancy as a Motivating Force', *Academy of Management Review*, **6**, pp. 589-99.

Sekaran, U. (1981), 'Are US Organisational Concepts and Measures Transferable to Another Culture? An Impartial Investigation', *Academy of Management Journal*, **24**, No. 2, pp. 409-17.

Selznick, P. (1949), *TVA and the Grass Roots*, Berkeley, University of California Press.

Selznick, P. (1957), *Leadership in Administration*, New York, Harper & Row.

Shrivastava, P. (1983), 'A Typology of Organisational Learning Systems', *Journal of Management Studies*, **20**, No. 1, pp. 7-28.

Silverman, D. (1970), *Theory of Organisations*, London, Heinemann.

Silverman, D. and Jones, J. (1976), *Organisational Work*, London, Collier Macmillan.

Simon, H.A. (1945), *Administrative Behaviour*, New York, Free Press.

Skinner, B.F. (1972), *Beyond Freedom and Dignity*, London, Jonathan Cape.

Smircich, L. (1983), 'Concepts of Culture and Organizational Analysis', *Administrative Science Quarterly*, **28**, pp. 339-58.

Sofer, C. (1961), *Organization from Within in What Causes Climate*, London, Tavistock Publications.

Sofer, C. (1970), *Man in Mid-career: A Study of British Managers and Technical Specialists*, Cambridge, Cambridge University Press.

Springer, J.F. and Gable, R.W. (1980), 'Dimensions and Sources of Administrative Climate in Development Programs of Four Asian Nations', *Administrative Science Quarterly*, **25**, pp. 671-88.

Stamp, G. (1981), 'Levels and Types of Managerial Capability', *Journal of Management Studies*, **18**, No. 3, pp. 277-97.

Stanton, E.S. (1980), 'Company Policies and Supervisors Attitudes Towards Supervision', *Journal of Applied Psychology*, **44**, pp. 22-6.

Staw, B.M. (1977), *Two Sides of Commitment: The Rational and Irrational Components of the Commitment Process*. Paper presented at the Annual Meeting of the Academy of Management, Orlando.

Stewart, R. (1967), *Managers and their Jobs*, London, Macmillan.

Stinchcombe, A.L. (1965), 'Social Structure and Organisation'. In March, J.G. (ed), *Handbook of Organisations*, Chicago, Rand McNally, pp. 142-93.

Stopford, J.M. (1973), 'Organizational Development in the Multi-national Enterprise'. In Graves, D. (ed), *Management Research: A Cross-cultural Perspective*, Amsterdam, Elsevier.

Strasser, S. *et al.* (1981), 'Conceptualising the Goal and System Models of Organisational Effectiveness', *Journal of Management Studies*, **18**, No. 3, pp. 321-39.

Strauss, G. (1974), 'Adolescence in Organization Growth', *Organizational Dynamics*, **2**, No. 4, pp. 3-17.

Super, D.E. (1953), 'A Theory of Vocational Development', *American Psychologist*, **8**, pp. 185-90.

Sutton, R.I. and Rousseau, D.M. (1979), 'Structure, Technology and Dependence on a Parent Organization: Organizational and Environmental Correlates of

Individual Responses', *Journal of Applied Psychology*, **64**, No. 6, pp. 675-87.

Tagiuri, R. (1968), 'The Concept of Organizational Climate'. In Tagiuri, R. and Litwin, G.H. (eds), *Organizational Climate*, Boston, Harvard University Press.

Taylor, J.C. and Bowers, D. (1972), *Survey of Organizations: A Machine Scored Standardization Instrument*, Ann Arbor, University of Michigan, Institute for Social Research.

Terborg, J.R. (1981), 'Interactional Psychology and Research on Human Behaviour in Organizations', *AMA Review*, **6**, No. 4, pp. 569-76.

Thomas, W.I. (1931), *The Unadjusted Girl*, Boston, Little, Brown.

Thompson, J.D. (1967), *Organizations in Action*, New York, McGraw Hill.

Thurley, K.E., Graves, D. and Hult, M. (1975), 'An Evaluation Strategy for Management Development', *ATTITB Training Research Bulletin*, **6**, No. 2, pp. 3-17.

Thurley, K.E. (1983), 'Comparative Studies of Industrial Democracy in an Organizational Perspective'. In Wilpert, B. and Sorge, A. (eds), *Industrial Democracy Handbook, Vol. 2* (forthcoming).

de Tocqueville, A. (1958), *Journeys to England and Ireland*, London, Faber & Faber.

Trist, E.L. and Bamforth, K.W. (1951), 'Some Social and Psychological Consequences of the Longwall Method of Coal-getting', *Human Relations*, **4**, No. 1, pp. 3-38.

Tung, R.L. (1978), 'The Use of the Organizational Construct in Comparative Management Models', *Academy of Management Proceedings*, 38th Annual Meeting, pp. 292-6.

Van Maanen, R. (1977), *Organizational Careers: Some New Perspectives*, New York, John Wiley & Sons.

Vroom, V.R. (1964), *Work and Motivation*, New York, Wiley.

Wales, J. (1980), 'A Four-culture Model of Collaborative Learning and Problem-solving, *Management International Review*, **20**, No. 4, pp. 100–11.

Wanous, J.P. (1980), *Organizational Entry: Recruitment, Selection and Socialization of Newcomers*, Reading, Mass., Addison-Wesley.

Watson, T.J. (1963), *A Business and Its Beliefs*, New York, McGraw Hill.

Weinshall, T.D. (ed) (1977), *Culture and Management*, London, Penguin Books.

Weinshall, T.D. (ed) (1979), *Managerial Communication*, London, Academic Press. See especially Chapters 7 and 9.

Whyte, W.H. (1957), *The Organisation Man*, London, Jonathan Cape.

Wiener, Y. and Vardi, Y. (1980), 'Relationships Between Job, Organization and Career Commitments and Work Outcomes: An Integrative Approach', *Organizational Behaviour and Human Performance*, **26**, pp. 81-96.

Wilkins, A.L. (1983), 'The Culture Audit: A Tool for Understanding Organizations', *Organizational Dynamics*, Autumn, pp. 24-38.

Wilkins, A.L. (1984), 'The Creation of Company Cultures', *Human Resource Management*, **23**, No. 1, pp. 41-60.

Wolfe, D.M. and King, D.C. (1976), 'Organizational Climate: Science or Folklore?', *Academy of Management Review*, October, pp. 816-26.

Woodward, J. (1965), *Industrial Organization: Theory and Practice*, Oxford, Oxford University Press.

Wuthnow, R., Hunger, J.D., Bergesen, A. and Kurzweil, E. (1984), *Cultural Analysis*, Boston, Routledge & Kegan Paul.

Index

(Note: *passim* means that the subject so annotated is referred to in scattered passages throughout these pages of text. 'T' indicates a table and 'f' a figure.)